DATE DUE

NO 4 90		
JE 22 '95		
NV 2 5 99		
JE 6 00		
JE 11 03		

DEMCO 38-296

TARGET:

The U.S. Asian Market

A Practical Guide to Doing Business

Angi Ma Wong

**PACIFIC
HERITAGE
B☯KS** P.O. Box 3967, Palos Verdes, California 90274-9547

Published by Pacific Heritage Books
Copyright © 1993 by Angi Ma Wong

International Standard Book Number 0-9635906-9-3
includes index.

Printed in the U.S.A.

First Edition: April 1993

Library of Congress Catalog Card Number 93-83449

Wong, Angi Ma

TARGET: THE U.S. ASIAN MARKET
   A Practical Guide to Doing Business

Other publications by Angi Ma Wong:

-Sane Motherhood © 1982
-The Practical *Feng Shui* Chart © 1992,

The following trademarks appear in this book: Coca Cola, Pepsi Cola, Weejuns, Bass, Hyundai, Korbel, Mercedes Benz, Remy Martin, The College Board,

Grateful acknowledgment is given to Asian Week, The Asian American Market Report, The Los Angeles Times, KSCI, Lennie Copeland (Plume), Roger Axtell (John Wiley and Sons), Philip Harris and Robert Moran (Gulf Publishing), Evelyn Lip (Heian), Derek Walters (Aquarian) for permission to reprint previously published material.

Cover design by Cheryl Solheid
Production services by Brian Staples, S^2 Productions, San Diego, California

To my parents Shui Tong and Renee Ma, David and Lillian Wong, and my grandparents
who empowered me with their love and an appreciation of the past

To my husband Norman
who for twenty five years has been the wind beneath by wings and
my present

To my children Jason, Wendy, Jamie, and Steven, and all their contemporaries
who are the international citizens of the future

DISCLAIMER

This book is designed to entertain and educate by providing information in regard to the subject matter covered. Although the author and publisher have researched many sources to ensure the accuracy and completeness of the information contained in this book, we assume no responsibility for errors, inaccuracies, omissions or any other inconsistency herein. This book should only be used as a general guide and not as the ultimate source of intercultural marketing information. It is sold with the understanding that the publisher and author are not engaged in rendering legal, accounting, or other professional services. If legal or other expert expert assistance is required, the services of a competent professional should be sought. The author and Pacific Heritage Books assume no liability or responsibility to any person or entity with respect to any loss or damage caused or alleged to be caused directly or indirectly by any use of the information contained in this work. Any slights against people or organizations are unintentional.

AUTHOR'S NOTE

For convenience only, the term "Asian" in this book will generally refer to those who were born in an Asian country, and may include visitors, students, business persons, and first-generation Americans. "Asian American" will identify second, third, fourth, and fifth generation Americans of Asian ancestry. Currently, there is much discussion among those of Asian ancestry as to what the nomenclature should be. Even among themselves, there exists a vast range of opinions on this topic.

SRI Research Center Inc./Gallup of Lincoln, Nebraska conducted polls of Vietnamese, Chinese, Korean, and Japanese American consumers. The findings:

70% of the Vietnamese identify themselves as "Vietnamese"
6% identify themselves as "Vietnamese Americans"

62% of Chinese Americans identify themselves as "Chinese"
11% identify themselves as "Chinese Americans"

71% of Korean American heads of households identify themselves as "Koreans"
23% identify themselves as "Korean Americans"

26% of Japanese heads of households identify themselves as "Japanese"
41% Japanese American heads of households identify themselves as "Japanese Americans"

ACKNOWLEDGMENTS

Had I not been diagnosed with cancer in the spring of 1989, this book may never have come into being. The shattering news, followed by six months of concurrent chemotherapy and radiation, was only one of many emotional upheavals I experienced that year. But when the turmoil had subsided, my consulting and seminar business had been launched and I had acquired an entirely new, proactive view of life.

My gratitude goes to the many friends and colleagues who have shared their time and knowledge to the production of this book: Angi Navarro, Aziz and Fatima Lakhani, Wanda Chang, David Sugita, Jim and Linda Esserman, Pauline Ampaiporn Hamwarangkul, Jackie Law, Mona Porotesano, Swan Ngin, Ben and Avery Hallowell who led me to Cheryl Solheid and Brian Staples, and to Dick Hamm who referred me to Patty Walsh, from whom I have learned much about the book business.

My editors Maxine Young, Tobie Gurewitz, and Tom McFadden deserve special thanks and appreciation, as does my computer support team, Adrian Lee and Tony Salso, both of whom exhibited infinite patience with my efforts to master a certain word processing program in order to write the manuscript. Thanks also, go to Marion and Gary Gray, my word processing "clean-up" crew.

Finally, I thank my family for all the stolen hours during which I was distracted with this project. Every moment dedicated to this book was precious time spent away from each of them, and for this I ask their forgiveness.

ABOUT THE AUTHOR

For over fifteen years before "multi-cultural education" became a buzz word, Angi Ma Wong was delighting audiences of all ages with her interactive presentations on the history and contributions of the Chinese to the development of the American West.

Ms. Wong enrolled as an architecture major at Virginia Polytechnic Institute and State University. As a junior, she became the founding president of Chi Delta Alpha, the university's women's service organization which in 1992 celebrated its 25th anniversary. She is a graduate of the University of Southern California and completed post-graduate studies at California State University at Long Beach and the University of California at Los Angeles.

As a founding member and past president of the Chinese Historical Society of Southern California, Ms. Wong has been honored by the Los Angeles City Council for her contribution to multi-cultural education and over twenty years of community service.

In 1989 Ms. Wong coined the term "intercultural consultant" and formed her own business providing training seminars and consulting services to facilitate improved communications between Asians and non-Asians. Since then her clientele has expanded to include over thirty major home developers in the West as well as retail businesses, financial and educational institutions, medical corporations, public relations and marketing companies, architectural firms, and non-profit organizations.

A community activist and businesswoman, Angi Ma Wong is a successsful lecturer and consultant who has authored numerous articles on a variety of subjects. She has presented at UCI, UCLA, California State University, Harbor College, and for the American Woman's Economic Development Corporation and the National Association of Women Business Owners. In addition, her diverse audiences range from the California Association of Hostage Negotiators and the Brain Injury Symposium, to the California Lab Managers Association.

In 1992 she developed The Practical *Feng Shui* Chart © kit, an educational tool based on the ancient Chinese art of placement.

PREFACE

For all the businesses that have seen the changing
   demographics and are flexible and visionary enough to move into new markets

For all of you who wanted a practical resource book on how
   to successfully conduct business with Asian Americans and Asians in the United States

For all the entrepreneurs who like myself have dared to
   venture into unchartered directions

For all those who tried to sell income, commercial, or residential property or
   anything to an Asian prospect, failed, and never knew why

For all of you who thought my seminars were too short

For those who kept asking in which bookstore this book could be found

For all the participants in my seminars who got writer's cramp from taking notes

For Mieke Eoyang who wanted Aunty Angi's business book to be "easy to read"

THIS ONE'S FOR YOU.

Angi Ma Wong

International business is like a handshake -

each of us must extend a hand halfway

until we touch, then synergize.

-Angi Ma Wong

TABLE OF CONTENTS

PART I

AMERICAN BREAKFASTS AND *KARAOKE* NIGHTS: THE MARKET YOU CAN'T IGNORE

The rise in Asian Pacific Islander population · Realizing the potential ·

Asia as a salad bowl · Statistics on 15 Asian countries · Origins of Asian stereotypes · The importance of knowing your market segment · Immigrants and refugees · Starting with the Yellow Pages (theirs) ·

Sources of Asian marketing information · List of colleges and universities with Asian studies departments · Other publications · Hiring professional help ·

PART TWO

INTO THE ASIAN MIND: REMOVING THE MYSTIQUE

The five relationships · Conformity · The influence of the family · Education and its impact on the family and society ·

Frugality · A different view of payola · War stratagems applied to Asian business · Bargaining · Successful negotiations · Spending their money · The $225 billion consumer group · Banks and loan clubs ·

PART THREE

BUSINESS ETIQUETTE AND COMMUNICATIONS

PART ONE

AMERICAN BREAKFASTS AND KARAOKE NIGHTS

The Market You Can't Ignore

CHAPTER ONE

THE HIDDEN BONANZA

It was the best-kept secret of the 1980's, but the clues were all there.

Insurance agents, retailers selling Steinway pianos, Mercedes Benz sedans, and $110 bottles of Remy Martin cognac noticed it first. So did many school districts.

Then during the recession that began in 1990, the homebuilders in California observed the same interesting trend. A great number of the people who were buying new homes were of Asian descent.

The magazine **American Demographics** published " **A New Look at Asian Americans**" in October 1990. Shortly thereafter, the report of the U.S. Census Bureau was published and the cat was out of the bag. In ten years, the 3.8 million people of Asian and Pacific Islander descent in the United States had mushroomed to 7.3 million strong. The 107% increase (127% in California) made them the fastest-growing group in the nation.

This tremendous increase began shortly after 1965, since it was in that year the Immigration and Nationality Act replaced the national origins quota system that formed the basis of Asian immigration.   Before 1965, immigration had been suppressed by unfair and discriminatory legislation culminating with the Chinese Exclusion Act of 1882.

This law was re-enacted nine times and was broadened to encompass other Asian groups besides the Chinese. It was repealed in 1943, only to be replaced by the national origins quota system. Under this system, only 105 ethnic Chinese, for example, were permitted to immigrate to the U.S. each year, at a time when thousands of Europeans were entering through Ellis Island in New York.

The 1990 census revealed the impressive growth in both Asian population and businesses. One could not help but sit up and take notice for much of what was learned was significant and often surprising. Until the 1970s, most Asians in this country were either of Chinese or Japanese descent, for they were the first Asian immigrants to arrive as early as 1788, at what was later to become one of the United States-Hawaii. In the past two decades or so, however, the trend has reversed: foreign-born Asians in the United States now outnumber Americans of Asian ancestry.

If the present course of immigration continues, 4.2 million more Asians will move to the United States in the next decade, totalling 17.1 million by the year 2010 and 34.5 million by 2040, representing 5.7% and 9.7% of the population respectively. From 1981 to 1989, almost half of all immigrants to this country originated from the Asian continent: 1.6 million Chinese, 1.4 million Filipinos, 848,000 Japanese, 815,000 Indians, 799,000 Koreans, and 615,000 Vietnamese.

Not surprisingly, over half of these newcomers reside in the Western states. Asians moving to California are projected to number 90,000 a year, totaling 4.5 million by the year 2000. Asian and Pacific Islanders outnumber African Americans in ten states (Maine, New Hampshire, Vermont, California, Hawaii, Idaho, Montana, Oregon, Utah, and Washington), and outnumber Hispanics in three (Maryland, Alaska, and Hawaii).

In California, Asians are the state's second-largest minority, numbering 2.8 million. New York, Hawaii, Texas, Illinois, New Jersey, Washington, Virginia, Florida and Massachusetts followed with the largest Asian populations in the country. The Chinese, Filipinos, and Japanese are the most numerous, followed by Indians, Koreans, Vietnamese, Cambodian, Hmong, Laotian, and Thai.

Why this is all very interesting, you may say, but I live in New Hampshire, an entire country's breadth away from California and the Pacific Ocean from where these numerous new immigrants are coming.

But even in those states where the percentage of Asians is relatively low, their impact is significant. For instance, New Hampshire's Asians earn among the highest income in the United States:

Top 5 States
Asian Pacific Islander - Median Household Income

New Jersey	$52,846
Connecticut	$48,560
Maryland	$45,446
New Hampshire	$42,963
Virginia	$41,488

The figures are enough to make any marketer drool. In some geographic areas, Asian and Pacific Island households out-earn white households by 23.1%, Hispanic households by 72.2%, and African American by 105.9%. On the West Coast, Asian homeowners in 1989 outearned whites by $4,000 annually ($50,010) compared to the total U.S. income of $35,480. In Southern California, 74% of Japanese Americans and 60% of Chinese Americans own their own homes. In Orange County, for example, home sales in 1991

Gifts for the family and household are popular during the Korean Harvest Festival. These include gift certificates, housewares such as linens, small appliances, kitchenware, new clothes for children, and gift certificates. Fruit and rice cakes as well as bounties of harvest decorate family tables.

reflected the pocketbook power of Asians: Asian surnames of home buyers occupied six of the top fifteen positions. For example, the top slot was occupied by the name Nguyen (456 homes purchased); second place was Lee (254 homes purchased); Smith occupied third place with 218 homes; in fifth place on the list was the surname Kim (162 homes). As the highest income-earning group of the four, they represent over *$225 billion* in purchasing power, compared to the $8.2 billion of the 22 million Hispanics in the U.S.

Median Household Income by Race
1990 Census-Geographical Area

	New England	Middle Atlantic	East North Central	West North Central	South Atlantic	East South Central	West South Central	Mountain	Pacific (includes Alaska & Hawaii)
Total U.S.	$36,241	$32,869	$28,706	$27,128	$29,281	$23,098	$25,267	$27,742	$34,428
White	36,990	34,814	31,448	27,709	31,325	25,424	27,570	28,921	35,710
Black	26,324	24,023	19,176	18,244	20,333	13,917	15,279	21,256	25,884
American Indian, Eskimo, Aleut	23,806	22,273	21,011	15,272	22,675	19,222	19,213	14,917	25,352
Asian Pacific Islanders	36,620	38,921	35,835	23,386		27,267	29,215	27,608	39,030
Hispanic	21,948	23,547	27,182	23,827	25,927	22,803	19,327	20,959	27,931
Other	19,078	20,420	25,602	22,598	24,865	21,908	19,083	20,534	26,432

Source: U.S. Bureau of the Census

The reasons for the higher household income are twofold. First, Asians in general have more education, resulting in higher-paying jobs. For example, among U.S.-born men aged 25-40, non-Hispanic whites average 12.86 years of education, whereas those of Chinese descent average 14.90 years. Among foreign-born non-Hispanic males of the same age group, the average number of years of schooling was 12.77, in sharp contrast to the 16.65 years for the Asian Indian male.

The second reason is that Asian families tend to have more wage-earners per household, many of which are business owners. 80% of all Koreans residing in the United States own their own businesses, resulting in a large group with considerable financial clout. The Korean-American Grocers Association, located in the City of Cerritos, California claims to represent 17,000 businesses worth $13 million in yearly sales.

Employment Status By Race
U.S. Census 1990 — 16 and over

	Total labor force (percent of population)	Armed Forces	Employed Civilians	Unemployed Civilians (percent)
Men	68,509,429 (74.4 %)	1,523,228	62,704,579	4,281.622 (6.4%)
Women	56,672,949 (56.8)	185,700	52,976,623	3,510,626 (6.2)
White men	56,853,639 (75.2)	1,154,530	52,722,444	2,976,665 (5-3)
White women	45,947,179 (56.3)	120,552	43,515,117	2,311,510 (5.0)
Black men	6,512,136 (66.5)	264,597	5,392,515	855,024 (13.7)
Black women	6,901,351 (59.5)	53,709	6,015,288	832,354 (12.2)
American Indian* men	472,266 (69.4)	12,374	388,911	70,981 (15.4)
Am. In. women	393,437 (55.1)	2,017	340,042	51,378 (13.1)
API** men	1,957,801 (75.5)	38,803	1,820,689	98,309 (5.1)
API women	1,688,145 (60.1)	4,063	1,590,897	93,185 (5.5)
Hispanic men	5,993,384 (78.7)	105,204	5,312,330	575,850 (9.8)
Hispanic women	4,145,686 (55.9)	12,143	3,669,186	464,357 (11.2)
Other (men)	2,713,587 (80.1)	52,924	2,380,020	280,643 (10.5)
Other (women)	1,742,837 (55.5)	5,359	1,515,279	222,199 (12.8)

* American Indian includes Eskimo and Aleut
** API: Asian Pacific Islander

Source: U.S. Bureau of the Census

Regardless of what kind of business you're in, you need to be attentive to the Asian market. Are you a health care provider? You'd be interested in knowing that many Asians are in need of your services.   Asian Health Services of Oakland, California recently published a report identifying this need.   Bilingual interviews revealed the following about the Asian community there:

22% men	Never had blood pressure taken
10% women	Never had blood pressure taken
71% men	Never had cholesterol measured
45% women	Never had a PAP smear
75% women	Never performed a breast self examination
68% women	Never had a mammogram

If you're in the grocery, food, beverage, restaurant, health/ or life insurance business, read on! The Korea Times, based in Los Angeles, conducted a study based on 600 randomly selected subjects with Korean surnames. Among its findings:

61.5%	Go to a Korean restaurant when dining out
23%	Go to a Chinese restaurant when dining out
77%	Drink at least one cup of coffee a day
	(77.4% prefer regular over 21.3% decaf)
56.4%	Prefer to drink Korean tea over standard tea
37.2%	Smoke (males)
20.5%	Smoke (females)
62%	Drink alcoholic beverages (men)
	(93.8% Catholic men drink; 51.3% Protestant men)
39%	Drink alcoholic beverages (female)
54%	Own life insurance
54%	Own medical insurance
49.8%	Own their homes

The 1992 **Japanese Directory and Guide** (Southern California) devotes an impressive number of pages in its back section to often-used information important to those of this ethnic group. Has your business been overlooking a major hidden market?

Number of pages	Topic
12	Medical terminology/health/AIDS
3	Size/measurements for clothing
5	Animals/foods
6	Restaurants (by kind)
6	Libraries
33	Golf courses (in the following counties: Los Angeles, Orange, Imperial, Kern, Riverside, San Bernardino, San Diego, Santa Barbara, San Louis Obispo, Ventura
17	Driving/licenses/driver's test
7	Automobile maintenance/car trouble
24	Las Vegas
8	Palm Springs
5	Ski
3	Fishing

Many businesses, awakening to the potential of these statistics, are now trying to tap into the Asian and Asian American market without fully understanding it, much less those who comprise it. The result is mistakes, wasted effort, time, and money. Why? Because these businesses assume that all Asians look alike, and that those who speak excellent English and seemed "westernized" or in appearance have completely adopted American cultures and values - a very wrong assumption.

Before realizing the potential of the Asian bonanza in the United States, businesses need to know more than the difference between <u>sushi</u> and <u>kim chee</u>, Sato and Seto, the ROC and PRC. A basic understanding of who these consumers are, from where they come, their lifestyles and values, will enable you and your company to better design, sell, market, and retain your clients and customers of Asian ancestry. At the very least, you can learn how to improve your business and social communications with them.   After all, they are your employers and employees, customers and colleagues, neighbors and friends, associates and family members.

Who are these energetic new immigrants who are breathing new life and energy into our sluggish economy and labor force? From where do they originate? What traditions and customs do they bring with them that distinguish them as consumers? What cultural factors impact their decision-making process? What do they buy, from where, and from whom?

Why should any business bother to spend the time and money to target such a relatively small consumer group? In order to survive during stagnant economic times such as those we have been in for the past three years, or at <u>any time</u>, companies must be constantly seeking new as well as non-traditional markets.   Moreover, although small in numbers, the Asian population in the United States represents billions of dollars in disposable income, just waiting to be reached.

Demographics indicate also, that while Asian Americans are mostly young now, they, like the general population of the U.S. is aging.

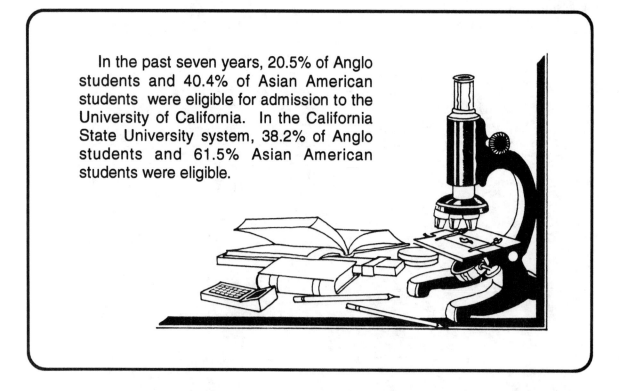

In the past seven years, 20.5% of Anglo students and 40.4% of Asian American students were eligible for admission to the University of California. In the California State University system, 38.2% of Anglo students and 61.5% Asian American students were eligible.

What businesses can tap into this hidden bonanza? **EVERY BUSINESS THAT WANTS TO,** including yours. Why? There are many opportunities that have been overlooked, and by doing a bit of digging, you can position yourself into a comfortable niche.

For example, in both the Japanese and Chinese business directories/yellow pages, there are absolutely no listings under "Tires". Why aren't major video and music chains such as The Wherehouse and Blockbuster Video listed under "Music"? Or why aren't B. Dalton or Bretano's, university or technical bookstores placing display ads under "Books"? Where are the names of medical centers such as Bellevue Hospital and the Mayo Clinic under the heading "hospitals"? Korbel airs beautifully-produced commercials with their voice-overs proclaiming "We have so much to celebrate". I think the company is missing a potential market by not including Asian wedding, birthday, or graduation scenes.

The more information you have, the more successfully you and your business can be reaching the U.S. Asian market regardless of whether you are based in Massachusetts, Vermont, Georgia, Florida, Wisconsin, or Hawaii. All of these states have experienced over 100% growth in their Asian populations in the past decades.

While many U.S. businesses are looking across the Pacific and investigating possibilities abroad, they may have missed the forest for the trees. As the old saying goes,"There's gold in them ther hills!" and the bonanza is right here at home!

CHAPTER TWO

AS ANNA SAID TO THE KING OF SIAM

It is crucial to your understanding of and potential success with the U.S. Asian market to have a basic knowledge of the origins of the millions of immigrants and refugees who have left their homelands to create new lives for themselves in the United States. The educational systems of many Asian countries teach a global view of geography while in America, the study of geography has virtually disappeared under the umbrella of "social studies." American students have earned the lowest scores in a geography test administered worldwide.

While your local library and bookstores probably have an exhaustive wealth of detailed information on every Asian Pacific nation, this chapter provides a quick look at just some of the major contributors to non-Caucasian immigration to and trade with America.

For starters, Asia is not one country or even one place. Broadly defined, it is an area between Europe and North America comprised of forty one countries, twenty five in or on the Pacific Ocean. It sprawls from Persia (Iran) to the west and Hawaii to the east and includes roughly half of the world's population.

In the ancient world, commerce, conducted by peoples of many races, coverged in Asia, and then dispersed to all corners of the world. China, with its many centuries of history, unabashedly called itself "Middle Kingdom," for it considered itself the center of the world; its hundreds of inventions and discoveries would later impact the Western world.

Asia consists not only of familiar names such as Taiwan, Hong Kong, Japan, India, Korea, Thailand, Indonesia, the Philippines and Malaysia, it includes names that you would ordinarily read only in travel brochures: Fiji, Borneo, Brunei, Papua New Guinea, and the Marshall Islands, to name just a few. Each of these countries has its own history, government, minority groups and tribes, languages and dialects, customs, traditions and culture.

Most Americans of Asian ancestry and Asians in the United States trace their ethnic origins to about a dozen countries. The following list will provide some basic facts regarding those.

CAMBODIA

-Area: 69,900 square miles
-Population: 6.8 million
-Type of government: Communist State
-Capital: Phnom Penh
-Languages:
-Literacy: 48%
-Ethnic makeup: Khmer 90%, Chinese 5%, other 5%
-Religions: Theravada Buddhist 90%, Catholic, Mahayan Buddhist, Islam
-Currency: Riel, $1 US=218.0 Riel
-Trade status with U.S.: minor
-No. in U.S.: 147,400
-Common surnames: Keo, Pheng, Thouch, Oum, Riem, Chanthan, Eng, Thong

CHINA, PEOPLE'S REPUBLIC

-Area: 3,691,521 square miles
-Population: 1.1 billion
-Type of government: Communist state
-Capital: Beijing
-Languages: Chinese, with more than eight major dialect groups
-Literacy: 75%

CHINA, PEOPLE'S REPUBLIC (continued)

-Ethnic makeup: Han Chinese 93.3%, others 6.7%
-Religions: None officially; Buddhist, Christian, Islam growing
-Currency: US$1 = 4.72 Renminbi yuan
-Trade status with U.S.: 14th largest trading partner
-No. in U.S.: 1.4 million (total Chinese)
-Common suranmes: Wong (also Huang, Hwang, Wang), Chang, Lee, Chen, Cheng, Fong, Liu, Hu, Lin, Sun, Leong (also Leung), Lum, Ho, Ma, Kung, Chung, Chao, Li (There are 5,662 Han surnames)

CHINA, REPUBLIC OF (TAIWAN)

-Area: 13,814 square miles
-Population: 19.8 million
-Type of government: One party dominant republic
-Capital: Taipei
-Languages: Mandarin Chinese, some English in metropolitan business areas
-Literacy: 94%
-Ethnic makeup: Taiwanese 84%, Mainland Chinese 14%, Aboriginal 2%
-Religions: Buddhism, Confucian, Taoist, Christian, Islam, others
-Currency: US$1 = NT $26.15 (New Taiwan dollar)
-Trade status with U.S.: 5th largest trading partner
-No. in U.S.: 1.6 million (total Chinese)
-Common surnames: (see list from preceding listing)

HONG KONG

-Area: 404 square miles
-Population: 5.7 million
-Type of government: British Dependent Territory, to revert to Chinese control on July 1, 1997
-Capital: Victoria
-Languages: Chinese (Cantonese dialect), English
-Literacy: 75%
-Ethnic makeup: Chinese 98%, other 2%
-Religions: Buddhist, Taoist, Christian
-Currency: US$1 = HK$7.87 (Hong Kong dollar)
-Trade status with U.S.: 10th largest trading partner
-No. in U.S.: 1.6 million (total Chinese)
-Common surnames: (see list under Peoples Republic of China)

INDIA

-Area: 1,269,420 square miles
-Population: 833 million
-Type of government: Federal republic
-Capital: New Dehli
-Languages: Hindi, English, over 17 other Indian languages and over 250 dialects
-Literacy: 36%
-Ethnic makeup: Indo-Aryan 72%, Dravidan 25%, Mongoloid & other 3%
-Religions: 80%+ Hindu, Sikh, Jain, Islam, Buddhist, Christian, Jewish
-Currency: US$1 = 16.96 rupees
-Trade status with U.S.: 24th largest trading partner
-No. in U.S.: 815,000
-Common surnames: Patel, Rao, Shah, Singh, Gupta, Mehta, Desai, Reddy

INDONESIA

-Area: 772,204 square miles
-Population: 187.7 million
-Type of government: Republic
-Capital: Jakarta
-Languages: Bahasa Indonesia, English
-Literacy: 62%
-Ethnic makeup: Javanese 45%, Sundanese 14%, Madurese 7.5%, Malay 7.5%, other
-Religions: Moslem 85%, 10% Christian, 5% Hindu (mostly in Bali, and Buddhist
-Currency: US$1 = 2,000. 00 Rupiah
-Trade status with U.S.: 27th largest trading partner
-No. in U.S.: 25,000 residents; 17,000 students (13,000 Students in California)
 (figures provided by Indonesian Embassy, Washington, D.C.)
-Common surnames: Hartanto, Wardoyo, Sugiarto, Subagio, Kusumaatmaja, Syarif,
 Suparman, Saleh, Panggabean, Nasution, Siregar, Harahap, Warouw, Mawengkang,
 Mailangkay, Yusuf.

JAPAN

-Area: 147,470 square miles
-Population: 123 million
-Type of government: Constitutional monarchy
-Capital: Tokyo
-Languages: Japanese, English in major metropolitan business areas
-Literacy: 99%
-Ethnic makeup: Japanese 99.4%, other 6%
-Religions: Shinto, Buddhist, some Christian

JAPAN (continued)

-Currency: US$1 = 143.5 Yen
-Trade status with U.S.: 2nd largest trading partner
-No. in U.S.: 847,500
-Common surnames: Sato, Suzuki, Nakamura, Takahishi, Ito, Watanabe, Saito, Yamamoto, Tanaka, Kobayashi, Kawaguchi

KOREA, REPUBLIC OF

-Area: 38,211 square miles
-Population: 42.7 million
-Type of government: Multiparty republic
-Capital: Seoul
-Languages: Korean
-Literacy: 93%
-Ethnic makeup: Korean
-Religions: Christian, Buddhist
-Currency: US$1 = 679.6 Won
-Trade status with U.S.: 7th largest trading partner
-No. in U.S.: 798,800
-Common surnames: Kim, Park, Lee, Chun, Ahn, Chang, Chin, Cho, Rho, Choi, Chung, Han, Koo, Lee, Lim, Oh, Park, Rhee, Rho, Whang, Yoon (Kim has 285 origins; Lee 241)

LAOS

-Area: 91,428 square miles
-Population: 3.9 million
-Type of government: Communist state
-Capital: Vientiane
-Languages: Laotian (polysyllabic); Hnong (monosyllabic)
-Literacy: 85%
-Ethnic makeup: Lao 48%, Kha 25%, Tribal Thai 14%, other 13%
-Currency: US$1 = 713.0 Kip
-Trade status with U.S.: minor
-No. in U.S.: 149,000 Laotian (lowland); 90,000 Hmong (mountain)
-Common surnames: Inatavong, Sananikone, Ly, Yang, Her, Moua
-(No trade with the U.S.)

MALAYSIA

-Area: 127,316 square miles
-Population: 16.5 million
-Type of government: Federal constitutional monarchy
-Capital: Kuala Lumpur
-Languages: Bahasa Malaysia, English, Chinese
-Literacy: 65%
-Ethnic makeup: Malay 59%, Chinese 32%, Indian 9%
  -Religions: Islam
-Currency: US$1 = M$2.699 (Malaysian ringgit)
-Trade status with U.S.: 23rd largest trading partner
-No. in the U.S.: (862 students in western region from Washington to New Mexico)
-Common surnames: (see Chinese and Indian names)

PHILIPPINES

-Area: 115,831 square miles
-Population: 61.5 million
-Type of government: Democracy
-Capital and major cities:
-Languages: Pilipino (Tagalog) and 67 languages and dialects, English, Spanish
-Literacy: 88%
-Ethnic makeup: Christian Malay 91.5%, Muslim Malay 4%, Chinese 1.5%
-Religions: Christian (90%+ Roman Catholic), Islam, Hindu, Buddhist, Jewish
-Currency: US$1 = 22.44 Philippine peso
-Trade status with U.S.: 26th largest trading partner
-No. in U.S.: 1.4 million
-Common surnames: Santos, Bautista, Reyes, de la Cruz, de Guzman, de los Reyes,
 Garcia, Martinez, Perez, Lopez,

SAMOA (American Samoa/Western Samoa)

-Area: 1,133 square miles
-Population: 38,000/157,408
-Type of government: U.S. administration/Constitutional monarchy under native chief
-Capital: Pago Pago/Apia
-Languages: Samoan, English
-Literacy: 90%
-Ethnic makeup: Samoan 88%, Euronesian 10%, other 2%
-Religions: Christian
-Currency: US$1/US$1 = 2.2 WS Tala (Western Samoa tala)

SAMOA (American Samoa/Western Somoa) (continued)

-Trade status with U.S.: minor
-No. in U.S.: 62,900
-Common surnames: Namulauulu, Papalii, Puilagi, Panuvasa, Fuimaono, Leilua, Seiuli, Ulugia

SINGAPORE

-Area: 239 square miles
-Population: 2.6 million
-Type of government: One-party dominant republic
-Capital: Singapore
-Languages: Chinese, Malay, English, Tamil
-Literacy: 87%
-Ethnic makeup: Chinese 76.4%, Malay 14.9%, Indian 6.4%
-Religions: Christian, Buddhist, Islam, Taoist, Hindu
-Currency: US$1 = S$1.90 (Singapore dollar)
-Trade status with U.S.: 12th largest trading partner
-No. in U.S.: N/A
-Common surnames: (Chinese, Malaysian, Indian, European)

THAILAND

-Area: 198,500 square miles
-Population: 55 million
-Type of government: Constitutional monarchy
-Capital: Bangkok
-Languages: Thai, English, Chinese, Malay
-Literacy: 82%
-Ethnic makeup: Thai 75%, Chinese 14%, other 11%
-Currency: US$1 = 25.69 Baht
-Trade status with U.S.: 25 largest trading partner
-No. in U.S.: 91,200
-(First names only are used): (Female) Amporn, Ampai, Anong, Pranee, Siriwan
 (Male) Somchai, Surasak, Prasong, Somsak, Prasit, Winai, Nipon, Pinit

VIETNAM

-Area: 127,207 square miles
-Population: 66,800
-Type of government: Communist state
-Capital: Ho Chi Minh City
-Languages: Vietnamese, French, Chinese, English
-Literacy: 78%
-Ethnic makeup: Vietnamese 85%, Chinese 3%, other 10%
-Currency: US$1 = 4,500 Dong
-Trade status with U.S.: Not a trading partner
-No. in U.S.: 614,500
-Common surnames: Nguyen, Pham, Phan, Tran, Le, Do, Troung, Ngo, Ho, Vo, Hoang, Dao, Dang, Duong, Dinh

A look at Asian lifestyles overseas will provide you with some insight to appreciate, literally and figuratively, "where they're coming from."

The countries, for the most part, are in the equatorial zone and therefore very hot, although there exist extremes in climate as well as geography. A great deal of humidity and rain is experienced throughout the year in all areas from India to the Islands of the Pacific. Those of you who have ever visited New York, Washington D.C. or New Orleans in the summer know how uncomfortable this combination can be.

There are a multitude of minority groups and languages within every country, and each has its own history, culture, customs and traditions. From family to family, village to village, district to district, province to province, dialects and surnames reflect the innumerable

Pacific Islander populations have also grown in the past decade. These include 211,014 Hawaiians (26% increase), 49, 345 Guamanian (53% increase), and 821,692 other Asian Pacifics (264% increase).

religious and ethnic subcultures. Because of labor shortages throughout Asia, there is much inter-country employment of nationals.

And yes, ethnocentrism, racial prejudice and discrimination is unfortunately alive and well in this part of the world too. To deny their existence would be to put our heads into the sand. Just as in the United States, manifestations can be as subtle as a snub or as blatant as laws directed at certain targeted groups. Violent acts have also been committed against various ethnic groups who are envied, feared or unwelcome.

There is a wide range of economic levels in Asia, just as there is here in the United States: the poor, destitute, homeless, and the obscenely rich, who live lavish and ostentatious lifestyles. It is not uncommon to see a chauffeur-driven Volkswagen "Beetle" in Hong Kong or school-aged children up to age 4 or 5 being hand-fed by a maid.

Asian cities are bustling, dynamic, extremely expensive, energetic, densely-populated, and very congested with vehicular as well as pedestrian traffic. A friend recently informed me that he paid 100% tax on his $100,000 German import automobile in Hong Kong. Another revealed that one square foot of space in downtown Tokyo is now valued at $225,000. And there are many stories going around about $100 taxi rides, $10 cups of coffee, and $500 hotel rooms in that same city.

It is no wonder that America is perceived as a bargain basement for the affluent of Asia who commonly go on shopping and golf junkets to the United States. To the very wealthy, the flight attendant's announcement of arrival at Los Angeles International Airport, probably translates to "Attention, K-Mart shoppers"!

Because cultures are deeply-rooted, so are their tribal or hierarchical traditions. Every child is brought up to know his or her position, rank, status, or caste in the community and society. Many of the rules that govern the society are unwritten, but nevertheless each person is constantly aware of, lives, and behaves in accord with them. Customs of meeting, forms of address, greeting, social and business relationships are dependent on the members of the society knowing exactly where his or her place is, or isn't.

The affluent and the noble therefore distinguish themselves by surrounding themselves with luxurious material goods and services that are beyond the reach of ordinary citizens. It is through signature clothing and jewelry, imported automobiles, fine liquor, the employment of domestic servants, global travel, multiple residences, etc. that they can proclaim their riches. When buying American, they prefer old, established, and well-known brands, but new products and services have a good chance if they quickly establish a good reputation for quality and value.

My father is a typical example of those who stick to the "oldies but goodies." Dad was born and raised in comfortable means in China, he attended one of the most prestigious universities in China,

The number of South Asians has increased since 1980 to 27,876 Pakastanis, 11,838 Bangladeshi, 10,970 Sri Lankan, 7,000 Fijians of Indian origin, and 7,000-10,000 Guyanese Indians.

and then Wharton School of Business at the University of Pennsylvania. He and Mom have lived in the United States for 32 years. When I was growing up, Dad always insisted on our buying Ford automobiles, Colgate toothpaste, and Hoover vacuum cleaners!

In many Asian nations, the middle class is the smallest in size and the agrarian/manual laborer class is largest in numbers. One either works with his hands for somebody, or is prosperous enough to hire somebody else to do the work for him. It is not uncommon to find a superior attitude among the well-heeled and a prejudice against those who are craftsmen or laborers. In the Chinese scheme of things, the jobs were ranked. At the top were the civil servants, farmers, trades/ craftsmen, merchants.

Because of the emphasis on education and the many levels of examinations to be passed to attain a civil post, that was the most respected position. Farmers contributed significantly to the basic survival of the populace, therefore were considered second in importance. Skilled craftspeople were relied upon for shelter, equipment, tools, and utensils and so occupied third place. At the bottom of the Chinese totem pole were the merchants and businesspeople, perhaps because they made money off everyone else.

Most people in the United States know what their own ethnic roots are. Asians and Asian Americans know theirs. Every one of us on both sides of the Pacific have our pride and prejudices. The cliché "All Asians look alike" is no more true than saying a Canadian resembles a Frenchman, or an Italian looks like a Greek. Funny thing, is, to many Asians, you look the "same" to them! And I must confess that even having lived around Asians on both sides of the Pacific all my life, I can correctly guess a person's Asian roots only about 60-70% of the time.

You can know ten things by learning one. - *Japanese proverb*

On a trip to San Francisco, I was walking through a shopping mall and saw a middle-aged Asian man trailing two younger men walking toward me. The man in front was impeccably dressed in a dark grey suit, white shirt, and a conservative tie. Behind him walked his two companions, presumably his sons. I couldn't suppress a chuckle as they passed. Both had hair that flowed halfway down their backs, streaked with orange. One was wearing a T-shirt printed with the skull-and-crossbones symbol of a popular heavy metal rock group; the other was clothed in an army shirt with the camouflage pattern. Both had on very baggy pants and their feet were shod in black army boots. All three men were representative of the Asian American market...the older and the younger.

Ham-and-egg mornings and *Karoke* (customer sing-a-long in night clubs) nights - the Asian consumer in the U.S. reflects two cultures: that of his or her origins and that of America. He or she is a fascinating mix of centuries-old traditions and customs laced with that of America, much like a chocolate marble cake.

To understand the U.S. Asian market, you must first do your homework and learn as much as you can about the various ethnic groups you are targeting. And after that, you will come to realize that while many commonalties are evident, there are some distinct differences. Knowing as much as possible about those differences can give you the advantage over your competition, as well as helping you to avoid costly mistakes in time and resources.

First and foremost to remember is also the most obvious - every single customer or client who walks into your place of business is an individual in his or her own right, whatever his or her ethnicity, gender, age, or nationality. Upon your first contact with a prospective customer, it doesn't matter at all to which of the various Asian groups the person belongs to, that person is *a potential client or customer.*

It may be helpful at this point to examine your own assumptions about Asians. Every one of us grew up with different backgrounds and lived in various parts of the world. Were there many Asians in your hometown or community? What positive or negative attitudes were expressed about Asians by your family members, neighbors, or friends regarding Asians? Have those attitudes colored your perceptions in any way? Do you have any associations with those of Asian ancestry now? As a businessperson, what can you learn from them? Can you overcome any prejudices, grudges, stereotypes, or opinions about Asians that you may have in order to do business with that group fairly and effectively?

Have you, or do you ever, say..........

· "I was in_____(name of Asian country) during the war."
· "My best friend is _____(name of Asian group".
· "Our son/daughter is married to an _____ ".
· "How long have you been in the United States?"
· "Your English is so good!"
· "You don't have any accent."
· "Say something in _____."
· "Where (what country) are you from?"

I daresay most adult Americans of Asian descent and new immigrant Asians have heard one or more of these at sometime or another. Some of us hear them more than others, especially if we don't speak with any accent. While I appreciate that some of these comments are made by non-Asians to relate to us and are attempts to be friendly, please understand that many Asian Americans find them to be boorish.

Stereotypes of Asians originated in the early days of their arrival here in the newspapers of the mid 1850's and were reinforced in film fifty to sixty years ago. Women were always portrayed as having long, black hair, wore kimonos or <u>cheongams</u>, the tight-fitting dresses with high collars and slits that exposed their thighs. Asian men dressed in black pajamas, and sported long, thin, drooping mustaches. Slanted eyes, coolie hats, round glasses and buck teeth often completed "the Asian look" in cartoons, caricatures, print and electronic media.

Some of the adjectives used to describe Asian men and women through the years are: heathen, stoic, mysterious, exotic, submissive, subservient, serene, complacent, don't make waves. In the 1800's, they were considered "the yellow peril" and always came in "hordes" or as an "invasion" to "our country". Even today, the term "foreign investors" always seems to evoke the image of Asians, when in fact, Canadian and British "foreigners" have until recently been the two major investors in the United States.

Movies such as "Charlie Chan", "Fu Manchu", "The World of Suzie Wong", "Mr. Moto", and "My Geisha" fired the imaginations of the American film-going public for decades and reinforced many negative and unrealistic stereotypes. An example is the long-running television series "Bonanza", popular in the late 50's and early 60's, which brought the character of Hop Sing, the Chinese domestic servant to the Cartwright family, into millions of homes every week. And of course, everyone "knows" that Asians could only be found in three occupations: restaurants, laundries, and produce.

The most common family name in the world is the Chinese surname **Chang**, with an estimated *104 million* members.

Accupressure, acupuncture as well as *cao gio* (coin rubbing) *be bao* (skin pinching) , *giac,* (cup suctioning), *xong* (herbal steam fumigation)**, balms, and herbs** are among many aspects of Asian traditional medicine.

Try this accupressure treatment for headache relief: Pinch hard on the fleshy mound between the thumb and index of your left hand between the thumb and four fingers of the right hand.

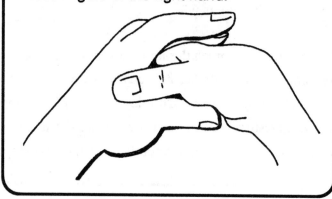

The perpetuation of these stereotypes has created a very thick "glass ceiling" in almost every profession, preventing highly-qualified, competent, and capable Asian Americans from achieving positions of rank in major mainstream companies and corporations. This topic continues to be researched, written about, and discussed in great detail over the years, but it appeared that little, if any progress, has been made to correct the situation. For example, there are thousands of Asian engineers and scientists who have dedicated their professional lives to the development of major aerospace and engineering corporations throughout the United States. Although many of them earn above-average salaries, their income still lags behind white Americans in similar occupations. Many of them are retiring without ever attaining management positions in the companies in which they loyally served for decades.

American participation in the Korean War, World War II, and the Vietnam War didn't help either. The experiences of servicemen with Asians overseas further muddied their perceptions or reinforced the stereotypes already held. The contacts between the military personnel on "R and R" leave and the general populace were mostly with the seedier elements of the local society. Moreover, the willingness of many Asian women to leave their countries and come to the United States as a G.I. or mail order bride did little to dispel their mystique and the myths surrounding them.

The concept of designing, marketing, and selling to ethnic populations is relatively new, but definitely worth your time and effort. By last count, there were over fifty Asian American marketing companies in the United States. One of the oldest, Lynne Choy Uyeda and Associates, for examples, was founded in 1984, and its president is the founding president of the newly-formed Asian American Advertising and Public Relations Alliance.

Today the **Asian American Journalists Association** and the **Association of Asian Pacific American Artists** based in Los Angeles seek to dispel such stereotypes in the printed and electronic media, act as monitors of legislation and mass communications, and assist in the realistic and accurate portrayal of Asian Pacific Americans. Another organization **Media Action Network for Asians (MANA)** is a non-profit, educational organization solely dedicated to advocating fair, accurate, balanced, and sensitive portrayals and news coverage of Asian Pacific Americans.

Treat your Asian or Asian American customer as you would any potential customer or customer...by providing superior quality and service, meeting his or her needs, and with fairness and dignity.

A poll taken of Asian consumers revealed the four most important factors in choosing a product were:

  (1) quality
  (2) price for value received
  (3) service provided
  (4) convenience

Come to think of it, these are not much different from the non-Asian consumer's choices, but there is one significant difference. The Asian American consumer appreciates your sensitivity and the effort to bridge the cultural differences between you. Items such as a brochure translated into his language from your retail store, helpful hints on home repairs from your hardware store, or how to properly prepare an income tax form from your accounting firm, a few decorations during the lunar new year or harvest moon celebrations will put you and your company on the cutting edge of your competition.

As a player in the U.S. Asian marketplace, you may need to separate and specifically focus on your target group. This means that within each group, there is a variety of combinations possible for you to sort out to avoid generalizing and to reach your market more efficiently. A case in point is the Japanese segment, which numbers approximately 850,000, mostly concentrated in two states: California (312,989) and Hawaii (247,486). The average age is 36; 20% are between the ages of 25 and 34; and 18% are under 25. Most have been in the United States for an average of twenty years. Their average household has three persons of which one is a student, and their income is in the $35,000 - $50,000 range. For 34% of these households, Japanese is the primary language.

Which part of this particular market would you like to reach? The answer depends largely on the length of time your audience has resided in the United States. In continuing our exploration of the Japanese component, we discover that Americans of Japanese ancestry have names: **issei** (first generation pioneers who arrived in the late 1800s), **nisei** (second-generation American of Japanese ancestry, over 100,000 of whom were sent to live in internment camps located throughout the western states during WWII), **sansei** (third generation Americans of Japanese ancestry) and **yongsei** (fourth generation Americans of Japanese).

Secondly, there are temporary residents (210,000 Japanese nationals who study or are employed in the United States and their dependents) or travelers (3.74 million in 1990 who spent an average of $3,516 during a U.S. trip in 1989).

Among the Japanese tourists, for example, a survey revealed that <u>safety</u> was their primary concern when traveling. Abiance, cleanliness, and a helpful staff followed in importance. These visitors love to shop, and spent an average $2,389 per trip to the United States. Their main dissatisfactions regarding their travels concerned food. The preferred soups, tea, and rice to our standard American fare. After the April 1992 civil disturbances in Los Angeles, Japanese tour companies promptly canceled tours, resulting in a projected $100 million in lost revenues.

"Know thyself, to know others, for heart beats like heart" a Chinese proverb declares. There are infinitely more commonalities between Asians and non-Asians than differences. Those cultural differences are not insurmountable and should not deter any business from addressing this hidden market.

There are three major differences between Asian and American cultures that you should be aware of: historical continuity, cultural identity, and ancestral pride. These are the origins of Asian values and attitudes, including education, family, religion, a sense of community, and their work ethic.

To say that Asian civilizations are very old is really an understatement. While our country is only 216 years young, the Chinese trace their roots back to the Wu Di period 2550 A.D. In 1992, the Chinese lunar year numbered 4690. Knowing this, you can appreciate that the dominant mentality of many Asians is one of <u>age</u>. It's the mindset difference between that of a youngster and his grandparents. The youth can be idealistic, impulsive, impatient, enthusiastic, naive, and lack the ability to think things through before acting. In contrast, his grandfather has lived three times as long, experienced the ups and downs of life, is more realistic, conservative, and maybe a bit skeptical.

All Asians, whether they are Americans or nationals from another country, are connected by their common culture. Images of the Tien An Men massacre in Beijing and Korean American-owned business going up in flames during the 1992 Los Angeles uprising are profoundly distressing. The pain of those experiences creates a deep affinity between fellow Asians.

However, the longer one's family has been in the United States, the more "Americanized" or acculturated a person becomes. Between 1990 and the year 2010, there will be a tremendous increase in the number of Asians in the age group of 45-64 for men, and   50-64 for the women. The same health and social problems that plague the aging, mainstream population will similarly affect Asian immigrant families that have rooted here for several generations. The statistics regarding divorce, crime, and cancer bear this out.

In the "old country," families lived in closed units, bound by tradition. A person's behavior was dictated by tribal or family norms. The Japanese saying "A nail that sticks out gets hammered down" is popularly quoted to teach that conformity was prized and any show of individuality or independent thinking was discouraged. In fact, up to the present day, a person who distinguishes himself from the crowd is generally considered not well-adjusted. This is in contrast to the American values of individualism, independence, self-sufficiency, and democracy.

The most powerful control came from within the family itself, as defined by basic Confucian tenets (Chapter Four). An individual couldn't make a move without automatically thinking of how his speech or behavior would reflect on those who shared his surname. If he did well on examinations, the entire unit could bask in his achievements; if he committed a crime, the entire family shared his humiliation and blame.

Business was conducted with a handshake, a "gentleman's agreement," supported by a family's honor and name, and commerce flourished by employing family members, rather than by hiring outsiders. A Los Angeles Times article dated July 22, 1990 details the formation and expansion of Chinese family networks on the Pacific Rim.

The difference between immigrants and refugees means a difference in your publicity efforts. Immigrants have made a conscious choice to leave their homes, live and work here, coming to join other family members who arrived earlier. Knowing a bit of the history of the Chinese in America, for example, will enable you to understand the general patterns of Asian immigration.

Asians are not new to this country. They have been coming to the United States since the first ninety Chinese blacksmiths and carpenters arrived on the <u>Felice</u> and <u>Iphigenia</u> in Maui 204 years ago. Families in Chinese towns and villages would pool their funds to pay for the ship passage of male relatives to come to America.

After their arrival, family and regional associations replaced the extended family units left behind. These associations would, among other activities, manage wages, send correspondence home, act as banker and mediator in legal or civil disputes, and if the worker came to an untimely death in America, arrange to have his bones shipped back to China for burial.

After the completion of the Transcontinental Railroad in 1869, a depression occurred, giving a dramatic rise in anti-Chinese legislation and sentiment. In 1882, the Chinese Exclusion Act prohibited the entry of Chinese laborers into the U.S., followed by the Scott Act six years later. The Scott Act stated that only Chinese professionals, scholars, merchants, students and visitors, were permitted to bring their families into this country.

Consequently, for 61 years until the Chinese Exclusion Act was repealed in 1943, over 20,000 men worked in our country without the benefit and companionship of their wives, children, and other family members. The legislation was instrumental in creating the "bachelor society", and eventually included all Asiatic peoples in its scope. Much has been written about these "sojourners" - these early pioneers who only came to work but had plans to eventually return to China. But many of those who were stranded here by the Exclusion Act were forced to remain in the United States for the rest of their lives, never to return home or see their loved ones again. Others ultimately married non-white women and settled as the first Asian immigrants here.

Most Asian immigrants today enter as immediate family members, of those who have come before them. This group usually has education, money, friends, and a network in place when they arrive. Their extended families offer moral and often financial support to help the newcomers get settled, very likely in the same community or neighborhood as their family.

Refugees, on the other hand, flee from their homes or countries to seek asylum from war or political persecution. The first large group of Asian refugees allowed into this country were 15,000 from Hong Kong in the early 1960's. By 1965, the Immigration and Nationality Act replaced the quota system and the doors were opened for other Asians to enter.

In 1975 after the fall of Saigon, the "first wave" of Southeast Asian refugees arrived in the United States. This group was characterized by their education, multi-lingual skills, and their association with European and American companies. In painful contrast are the "second wave," the refugees who may have been living in squalor in a refugee camp in Thailand, Indonesia, the Philippines, or Hong Kong for years before they are allowed to come to the U.S. Many have no marketable skills or financial resources and a great number of these "boat people" have encountered piracy, rape, and murder as they made their way to the United States. They may suffer from physical and psychological problems. In relocating to America, these refugees experience extreme forms of culture shock. In many communities that have refugee populations, community-based organizations have been established to assist them.

If a new Asian immigrant has resided in the United States for fewer than ten years, research indicates that he or she would be more likely to patronize a business that has advertised in his or her native language. In the San Francisco Bay area, Chinese is gaining ground over English. In a 1986 baseline survey of 778 Chinese respondents, 69% preferred Chinese over 29% who preferred English. But the **Asian American Market Report** reports that in July of 1991, 84% preferred Chinese over only 16% who chose English, a dramatic decrease. In San Francisco, the Cantonese dialect was preferred over Mandarin, 83% to 7%; in San Mateo, 57% preferred Cantonese, 19% preferred Mandarin, and 24% English.

Another example is the Filipino market, numbering almost 1.5 million in the country. A NuStats Inc. study conducted in Orange County, California, revealed that Tagalog was the primary language spoken in 71% of the households and English in 29%. However, if your target is immigrants who have lived in the United States for over ten years or are Asian Americans, you will do better to use mainstream marketing strategies in the English language. Where was your target customer educated, in his or her own country or here in the United States? A student who is a fifth-generation American of Japanese descent and a University of Michigan graduate requires a completely different marketing effort than a Taiwanese business executive who flies back and fourth across the Pacific ten times a year and is now looking for furniture for a home here in the States.

However, you may wish to advertise in telephone directories specifically directed toward the Asian market. Asian "yellow pages" year-round, you can. There are Asian yellow pages have proliferated to serve those in major cities where the Asian population has grown. Keep an open mind, do your own research, and you too, can tap into this public.   If you get a copy of the foreign language yellow pages in your community, you can determine whether your business could be listed. Considered cross-listing in several different categories. These yellow pages are usually distributed free and you'll probably find copies at the ethnic restaurants or markets. Just ask to borrow it for a moment, copy down the publisher's name and number, and call to find out how you can put your name and company at the fingertips of thousands of potential consumers.

Here is a sampling of the ethnic yellow pages across the nation:

Asian Yellow Pages

(3 directories; bilingual Chinese-English; Vietnamese/English; Japanese/English
Published by Direct Language Inc.
346 9th Street
San Francisco, CA 94104 Phone(415) 626-4111

Chinese Consumer Yellow Pages

Chinese Overseas Marketing Service Inc.
525 South San Gabriel Blvd.
San Gabriel, CA 91776
(818)285-6500 FAX (818) 285-7066

Chinese Yellow Pages and Business Guide

Published by Davis Media Group
1660 South Amphlett, Suite 122
San Mateo, CA 94402
(415) 573-7480 FAX (415) 573-9275

Chinese Yellow Pages and Business Guide (continued)

-Chicago; circulation 25,000
-Hawaii; circulation 35,000
-Houston; circulation 35,000
-Los Angeles; circulation 120,000
-San Francisco North Bay; circulation 50,000
-San Francisco South Bay; circulation 50,000
-Seattle; circulation 25,000
-Vancouver, British Columbia; circulation 35,000
-Washington, D.C.; circulation 25,000

South Bay (Southern California) Korean Business Directory

17813 South Main Street, #1120
Gardena, CA 90248
(310) 769-5722   FAX (310) 769-4903

Korean Business Directory

The Korean Central Daily
690 Wilshire Place
Los Angeles, CA 90005
(213) 389-2500   FAX (213) 389-6196
Circulation: 70,000

Korean Business Directory

Published by Korea News
42-22 27th Street
Long Island City, New York 11101
(718) 803-0909
Circulation: 4,000 (New York-New Jersey-Connecticut area)

The Japanese Telephone Directory and Guide (Southern California)

Published by Japan Publicity
120 South San Pedro Street, Suite 415
Los Angeles, CA 90012
(213) 617-1837   FAX (213) 617-7857

Yellow Pages Japan in U.S.A.

Yellow Pages Japan Inc.
420 Boyd Street, #502
Los Angeles, CA 90013
(213) 680-9101

CHAPTER THREE

INFORMATION ON THE ASIAN MARKET - WHO YA GONNA CALL?

As our country slowly drags itself out of the longest recession in history, those businesses that have bent like bamboo in the wind have survived. Others less flexible have broken and gone down. When the results of the 1990 U.S. census were published, many companies were not in a position to take advantage of the tremendous amount of data.

Some alert executives took notice of the changing demographics and quickly positioned themselves to be the first to move into Asian markets. Needless to say, these same companies are still tops in their industries today because they were about eighteen months ahead of everyone else. By utilizing their marketing research, providing sales training, and educating themselves, giants like William Lyon Company, Lewis Homes, Fieldstone, Kaufman and Broad, Home Savings of America were able to take the initiative in the Asian market. The following companies are also in the forefront of the U.S. Asian marketing race: MCI, AT&T, Anhauser-Busch, Cathay Pacific Airlines, Alladin Hotel and Casino, CIGNA, Hyundai, Japan Life America, Miller Brewing, Martell's Cognac, Steinway and Sons, Samsung Electronics, Thai

Airways, Charles Schwab, DHL Worldwide Express, Chivas Regal, Pacific Bell, Sprint, New York Life, Encyclopedia Britannica, Office Depot, PG&E, Sumitomo Bank, and Southern California Toyota dealers.

But what about those of you who are just realizing that the Asian market is one to be reckoned with? Is it too late? Where does a company start looking for information, especially for specifics regarding the U.S. Asian market? If you are not one of the biggies with a substantial budget and an entire department devoted to marketing research, where can you find sources of information?

Unfortunately, the best material is in newspapers - <u>foreign</u> language newspapers in 41 different Asian languages! Reportedly there were <u>70</u> newspapers in the Chinese language alone in the Southern California area! Check the yellow pages in your local and metro areas to see what's available locally.

Fortunately, there is much still available in English. Current news regarding Asian Americans can be found in **Asian Week** For a measly twenty-five bucks, you can subscribe to this newspaper for a year and keep up with the news, names, issues, and trends pertaining to Asian communities across the country. Three recent editions provided valuable statistics regarding Bay Area consumers, the growth in Asian and Pacific Islander population, and the Los Angeles Chinese and Vietnamese consumer markets. Somebody else paid for and did the research but you and your company can benefit from the results without your having to spend a bundle.

For example, did you know that over 40% of Bay Area Asians make over $40,000 a year? Or that Ajax, Toyota, Bank of America and Union 76 are preferred by Los Angeles Chinese Americans? Or that nearly two-thirds of all L.A. Vietnamese American households have VCR's, 23% have personal computers, and 15% shop at K Mart?

Remember that this is published in English and targets the Asian-American, not new immigrant market. **Asian Week** has also published *Asians in America 1990 Census* which can be purchased for $15. Don't overlook newspapers such as the **The Los Angeles Times**, **The Seattle Post Intelligence**, **The Wall Street Journal**, and smaller publications such as **The Orange County Register** which has conducted numerous surveys on the large Asian population in that area.

Rafu Shimpo, founded in 1903, is your best bet to stay knowledgeable about the concerns of the Japanese in the United States. This publication can provide valuable clues to what is of interest both in Japan and Stateside. For example a recent article announced the opening of L.L. Bean's first retail store in that country. Again, a trip to your local library can yield a much information about the Asians living in your community.

You will want to know that early post-census research was done by **KSCI Channel 18**. 40% of Vietnamese Americans and 33% of Chinese Americans surveyed indicated that they would be more likely to buy from a business that advertised in their native language. If you look in your local yellow pages you may be able to turn by marketing and public relations firms that specialize in the Asian sector. If not, call the **Asian American Advertising and Public Relations Alliance. AAAPRA** has over 50 members across the nation.

Everyone who does business with Asian Americans must have a copy of *Asian Pacific Americans*. For a mere five dollars, you can receive this 80-page booklet which was first published in 1989 and is into its second printing. Originally designed for use by members of the print and electronic media, this little gem is a learning primer for all of us, Asians and non-Asians alike. For example, Part 7 is 11 pages of demographics; Part 9 is a resource directory 20 pages long; Part 10 a directory of Asian Pacific news outlets.

If you want to know how many Asian-owned businesses are in Houston, what percentage of Asian Pacific Americans have college educations, or in which states reside two-thirds of the nation's Philipinos, then this little book is a valuable resource to keep handy. Never was the saying "Big things come in little packages" more true.

The photographs, copy, nationwide statistics, etc. in *Asian Pacific Americans* contribute greatly to dispelling myths, increasing awareness, and raising sensitivity to 19 different Asian Pacific ethnic groups. The book is the result of a combined effort of the National Conference of Christians and Jews, the Asian American Journalists Association, and the Associations of Asian Pacific American Artists in cooperation with over a dozen heavy-duty sponsors.

If you are operating in another state than California, you still can have access to much information. The **Asian American Market Report** is filled with current Asian market information in each issue, twelve times a year. For example, the March 1992 edition provides eleven resource directories for developing direct mail lists.

WELCOME TO
Krungthep Mahanakhon Bovorn Ratanakosin Mahintharayutthaya Mahadilokpop Noparatratchathani Burirom Udomratchani-vetmahasathan Amornpiman Avatarnsathit Sakkathattiyavisnukarmprasit

The full name for Bangkok, the capital city of Thailand, is the longest place-name in the world, although it is rarely used.

Other sources are weekly and monthly business publications, the U.S. Census Bureau, international, national, and regional print media such as the **Asian Wall Street Journal**, newspapers. Your local library can also provide you on the annual conferences, conventions, and seminars scheduled for your geographic area. These are concentrated gatherings of speakers and participants who are generally the foremost in their fields of expertise.

Ethnic NewsWatch, a subscription-based service which provides information about minority communities in the United States, is now offered by Softline Information of Stamford, Connecticut. It is currently available at the following university libraries: Harvard, Stanford, Columbia, Cornell, Berkeley, and the Universities of Pennsylvania, Michigan, Wisconsin, and California, as well as at the New York, San Jose, Boston, and Newark, New Jersey public libraries.

Yankelovich Monitor of Westport, Connecticut has published the **Asian American Monitor** based on the annual survey of 1,600 households in seven cities, and targeting the Chinese, Filipino, Japanese, Korean, and Vietnamese. Should you need demographic information pertaining to Asian health care, the **Verus Group** of Seal Beach, California can help you. Consult the appendix for other sources and resources.

An often overlooked resource is any university in the United States that has a department of Asian studies. Nationwide, the following is a list of institutions that have such programs. Are you and your business located in the proximity of any of the following? Utilize the brainpower nearby! (The number in parentheses indicates the state's Asian population and its percentage of growth since 1980 according to the 1990 U.S. Census.)

Arkansas (12,530; 85.9% increase)

Hendrix College

California (2,845,659; 127% increase)

Calif. State University, Long Beach
Claremont McKenna College
Laney College
Monterey Institute of International Studies
Naval Postgraduate School
Occidental College
Pitzer College
Pomona College
San Diego State University
Scripps College
University of California
    Berkeley
    Los Angeles
    Santa Barbara
University of the Pacific
University of Redlands

Colorado (59,862; 100.1% increase)

Colorado College
University of Colorado at Boulder

Connecticut (50,698; 167.3% increase)

Connecticut
Trinity College
Wesleyan University

District of Columbia (11,214; 120.3% increase)

Georgetown University

Florida (154,302; 171.9% increase)

Florida State University
Miami-Dade Community College
University of Florida

Hawaii (685,236; 17.5% increase)

Hawaii Loa College
University of Hawaii at Manoa
West Oahu

Illinois (285,311; 78.7% increase)

Augstana College
Illinois College
KAES College
Lake Forest College
Northwestern University
Principia College
University of Chicago
University of Illinois at Urbana-Champaign

Indiana (37,617; 83% increase)

DePauw University
Indiana University Bloomington
University of Notre Dame

Iowa (25,476; 120.1% increase)

University of Iowa
University of Northern Iowa

Louisiana (41,099; 72.8% increase)

 Tulane University

Maine (6,683; 126.8% increase)

 Bowdoin College

Maryland (139,719; 117.4% increase)

 Morgan State University

Massachusetts (143,392; 189.7% increase)

 Hampshire University
 Harvard and Radcliffe Colleges
 Mount Holyoke College
 Tufts University
 Wellesley College
 Wheaton College
 Williams College

Michigan (104,983; 84.9% increase)

 Eastern Michigan University
 University of Michigan
 Western Michigan University

Minnesota (77,886; 193.5 % increase)

 Carleton College
 St. Olaf College

Missouri (41,277; 78.7%)

 Washington University
 Westminister College

New Hampshire (9,343; 219% increase)

 Dartmouth College

New Jersey (272,521; 162.4%)

Rutgers-The State University of New Jersey
    Douglass College
    Livingston College
    Rutgers College
    University College New Brunswick
Seton Hall University

New Mexico (14,124; 106.9% increase)

University of New Mexico

New York (693,760; 123.4% increase)

Bard College
Barnard College
City University of New York
    Brooklyn College
    City College
Colgate University
Cornell University
Hamilton College
Hobart College
Hofstra University
Manhattanville College
St. John's University
St. Lawrence University
Sarah Lawrence College
State University of New York at Albany
Vassar College
William Smith College

North Carolina (52,166; 146.3% increase)

St. Andrews Presbyterian College
University of North Carolina at Chapel Hill

Ohio (91,179; 90.7% increase)

Bowling Green State University
Case Western Reserve University
Kent State University
Kenyon College
Ohio State University: Columbus Campus
Ohio University
Union Institute
University of Cincinnati
University of Toledo

Oklahoma (33,563; 94.3% increase)

Oklahoma City University
Phillips University
University of Oklahoma

Oregon (69, 269; 99.2% increase)

Northwest Christian College
University of Oregon
      Eugene
      Robert Donald Clark Honors College
   Williamette University

Pennsylvania (137,438; 113.5% increase)

Bucknell University
Gettysburg College
Penn State University Park Campus
Swarthmore College
Temple University

Rhode Island 918,325; 245.6% increase)

Brown University

South Carolina (22,382; 89.1% increase)

Furman University

Tennessee (31,839; 128.0% increase)

University of Tennessee: Knoxville

Texas (319,459; 165.5% increase)

Baylor University
Rice University
Southwest Texas State University
Trinity University
University of Texas at Austin

Utah (33,371; 121.4% increase)

Brigham Young University

Vermont (3,215; 137.3% increase)

Marlboro College
University of Vermont

Virginia (159, 053; 140.2% increase)

University of Virginia

Washington (210, 258; 105.7% increase)

University of Puget Sound
University of Washington
Washington State University

Wisconsin (53,583; 195.0% increase)

University of Wisconsin: Madison

American Territories

University of Guam

(sources: *The College Board: Index of Major and Graduate Degrees 1993, College Entrance Examination Board, New York, 1992* and U.S. Census Bureau)

Many universities have professors of Asian literature, culture, and Pacific Rim economics, on staff; some are experienced business people. Moreover, there are students attending classes, doing special projects, and working on various higher degrees, as well as already conducting research for and writing their doctoral dissertations. Many colleges and universities have business programs which focus on the Pacific Rim - these are also worth looking into for material. The Rose Institute of State and Local Government at Claremont - McKenna College is a case in point.

The Asian American Studies Center of the University of California, Los Angeles (UCLA), for example, has published ***Asian Pacific Community Directory of Organizations in Greater Los Angeles*** which contains over 400 listings (Asian American Studies Center, Student/Community Projects, 3232 Campbell Hall, UCLA). Does the college or university in your own community publish a similar directory that could be a springboard for your information search?

Do not overlook two other valuable resources - your <u>local</u> municipal governments, agencies and community-based organizations such as United Way. Many of them have already conducted studies, research analysis, and surveys of their own. If you live or work in an area that has a substantial Asian population, there is bound to be social service organizations, religious and/or cultural groups, professional organizations, and other resources. In July 1980, the Union of Pan Asian Communities, published ***Understanding the Pan Asian Client*** which gives an excellent overview of eleven major Asian/Pacific Islander groups.

A small crop of Asian-American targeted publications are available. ***Lifestyle USA*** is an example. It targets the approximately 210,000 Japanese nationals who have come to work in the United States. Another is ***Filipinas***, based in San Francisco. Its circulation is 10,100 and targets the Filipino segment in the Bay area. Don't stop here...what Asian American publications can you ferret out in your local community?

Your local yellow pages can be a valuable source of information if you look under the listings for organizations (e.g. professional groups) as well as ethnic chambers of commerce. More and more there are Asian American organizations forming for cultural, language, professional, and community activities. Don't overlook the resources at your local library which generally will carry much current data on the immediate community it serves, such as demographics. A reference librarian can be your best source of help when starting your search.

When you need to learn a lot in a hurry, it may be smart to just spend the money and bring on an expert to augment your in-house sales and marketing departments. This makes good sense, saves time as well as money, and may be cost effective. You can hire a consultant for several hours and get all the answers to the exact questions you want or train entire departments.

There is no way you can ever know as much as the expert because you and your company are too involved in the product development, planning timelines, meeting deadlines and beating out the competition. Most experts have spent their <u>lifetime</u> acquiring their knowledge, living and learning from mistakes and experience. Some maintain extensive networks, others are specialists, so it is wise to find out what background and experience he or she has before signing him/her on.

For example, an "intercultural consultant" may not be able to read your blueprints or work with your interior design team. While one's forte may be managing the multicultural workplace, she may not be the right person to train your sales team. A college professor may not be the best person to help you design an advertising or marketing campaign targeting the local Cambodian market, and so on. You get the general drift.

Last, but not least, do you personally know any Asians or Americans of Asian descent? If so, you could "pick their brains." The closer those neighbors, friends, associates, etc. are to your target market, the better. If you are willing to ask questions and listen to their responses, you can gain much valuable insight and use it to your advantage.

Finally, if you don't want to tackle your Asian marketing effort alone, you can hire a firm that has experience to help you. Since the early 1980's, over 50 Asian-owned marketing and public relations firms have sprung up. In April 1992, the Asian American Advertising and Public Relations Alliance held its kickoff reception in Los Angeles. This organization recognizes Asians in America as a viable market, promotes the standards of professionalism among Asian American practitioners in the fields of advertising, public relations, marketing and related industries.

A good consultant will help you to ascertain your specific needs and facilitate problem-solving for you and your company. Just as you may have done your own tune-ups on your jalopy back in your college days, today you wouldn't dream of messing around with the computerized fuel-injection system, so you wisely choose to take your automobile to an expert, a trained professional mechanic. Likewise, when you design a house, you hire professionals to do the job. You select an architect, a structural engineer, and call in a professional landscaper instead of going down to the local nursery, hardware, and garden shops to get all the tools and plants to do the job yourself.

Don't be penny wise and pound foolish - spend the bucks and save precious time and money to avoid costly cultural mistakes that may offend the very market you are targeting.

Notes

PART TWO

INTO THE ASIAN MIND

Removing the Mystique

CHAPTER FOUR

CONFUCIUS AND THE AGE OF THE PACIFIC

One man who impacts the way Asians do business and raise their families and has been dead for 2,500 year: Confucius, the Chinese scholar who lived between 551-479 B.C.   Two of his major maxims set forth guidelines for correct moral behavior. These have had a profound influence on the way Asians and Asian Americans conduct business and raise their families.

First, this philosopher and teacher believed that to maintain an orderly society, there must be regulation of the most basic of all human groupings, the family. Confucius laid down the rules of five unequal and dominant relationships to achieve this end.

a. Young people defer to older people
b. Son defers to his father
c. Younger brother defers to older brother
d. Wife defers to husband
e. Subject defers to ruler

This pyramid of influence still prevails today, profoundly pervasive in Asian societies and thousands of years after Confucius' death. While American culture glorifies youth, the Asian tradition for centuries has honored age for its experience and wisdom. The teachings of Confucius spread throughout the Asian continent, and his influence continues to be far-reaching.

These tenets established the last word on authority, accountability, and responsibility. Family members were under the onus of the eldest who kept his "ducks in line." A family's honor depended upon how well those with seniority could modify the behavior of its members to fit the social norms. Every word or action reflected upon one's family name and woe be those who brought shame or disgrace to it.

Asian children have been brought up for centuries conforming to societal standards. If a young man earned high marks on his examinations and was accepted to a respectable civil post that had potential for advancement, his entire family and village shared in the reflected glory of his accomplishments as well as the monetary rewards associated with it. On the other hand, if a child committed a transgression, he brought shame and embarrassment to his family, causing them to "lose face." In many instances, it may not even be a transgression, merely bringing attention to one's self.

In my multi-cultural in-service lectures to teachers, I am commonly asked why Asian children "fail to raise their hands in class and participate in class discussions." This "non- participation" is a manifestation of the "The nail that sticks out gets hammered down" principle. At home, the children may have been taught not to call attention of any kind to one's self or family, but to seek anonyminity in the masses. Moreover, calling attention to oneself (e.g. raising a hand in class) goes against the teaching of humility, one of the most prized virtues in Confucianism.

When an Asian student finally decides for himself that raising one's hand in class is an acceptable behavior, he ventures to do so. Envision the scenario. He may gingerly raise an arm and the teacher calls on him. Everyone in the class turns their attention on this chosen person, focusing their attention on him. Now the student has to "perform." If his answer is correct, great; if not, he has placed himself in a "face-losing" position. He has brought attention and embarrassment upon himself and may now feel guilt and anxiety for he has "shamed" his family, his relatives, everyone in his ethnic group, as well as all Asians! Now he is mortified and it may take some time for him to gain the confidence to raise his hand again.

Growing up in a Chinese home, this message was incessantly drummed into my own head, sometimes subtly and sometimes, not so subtly, by my parents and grandparents. You, Angi, must always do and act well, because you are representing the Chinese people. Even in the United States, you will be seen and judged as an Asian rather than as an American.

Books on communications bear this out, asserting that in the first 30 seconds of meeting, the impression a person is already making his or her impression. Ethnicity (color of one's skin), gender, and age are the first things that are assessed.

Confucius' principles embraced a respect for learning, culture, the past, and an orderly society based on hierarchy.

American values by contrast encourage and celebrate individualism, independence, and assertiveness, as well as the "I can do" mentality. We in America were brought up believing that we are in control of our lives and can make choices to effect changes. Traditional Asian thinking takes a more fatalistic approach, a belief in kismet or destiny, in a "que sera, sera, whatever will be, will be" attitude. Moreover, most Asian countries through the centuries have had authoritarian, often despotic rulers, not democracies to govern the populace. Thus, thinking for one's self, making individual decisions, and standing up for one's principles and beliefs was not the norm.

The second of Confucius' dictums which impacts us was the cornerstone of education: do not do or say anything that will cause hurt or embarrassment to another. Five hundred years before Christ, Confucius was already espousing the Golden Rule. The chain of authority coupled with this foundation of education created a rock-solid foundation for Chinese, and later other Asian families and society. It was a major task for each family authority to keep peace and order at home while maintaining the spirit of cooperation and harmony without avoiding confrontation and conflict.

In today's Asian communities, while the family is still the single most important motivating force in people's lives, westernization and acculturation have eroded the traditional structures. However, the blood ties and bonds are still incredibly strong and tightly knit. It is not uncommon for older family members to give financial help to favorite sons and daughters, nieces and nephews, single or married.

A well-brought-up young person will heed the advice of his elders before making any major decision. There is never any question as to who has authority or the final say about things: the older people always do. Sometimes this influence borders on control and may extend to many personal matters, including choosing of a university, profession, wife, or business.

I myself am a typical example of this type of influence. Years ago as a high school senior, I applied to and was accepted to Pratt Institute in New York where my mother had studied. I had great dreams and aspirations of having a career in art as a designer. This was not to be. My very traditional father remarked that "You can't make a living in art" and as an obedient Chinese daughter, I did the next best thing and enrolled as an architecture major at Virginia Polytechnic Institute.

While the elders do recognize that their offspring are now living and working in America and are becoming increasingly more Westernized, they do in their deepest of hearts wish that "My son would/should be a doctor," or "How come my daughter can't find a nice young man who speaks our language?" As the mother of an extremely bright, upcoming elected official once intimated to me wistfully years ago, "We had hoped that he would be a banker like his father, but he became a politician instead."

Education

It's no secret on both sides of the Pacific that education is what is propelling the Pacific Rim countries and their immigrants on the cutting edge of the world market. Consider the following sampling of literacy rates in the region:

Singapore	100%
Japan	99%
Taiwan	93%
Malaysia	90%

In contrast, the average reading level in the United States is at the 6th grade, down from 8th several years ago, and there are 25 million functionally illiterate Americans. Moreover, the high school dropout rate in this country is 30%, 40% in the Los Angeles United School District, the second-largest in the nation. It becomes apparent very quickly why we may be losing our lead in the world marketplace.

In the 1990s and beyond, economic might will be more powerful than military might. In the last few decades, a revolution has taken place - that of information. Our country cannot afford to deny to our young people the skills needed to survive in the global market. They will be required to acquire, transfer, analyze, sort, organize, and evaluate data of all kinds.

In order to do this, American students must have the basic skills to empower them to compete internationally. Basic skills, such as reading, writing, mathematics, speaking and listening, are crucial in communications, both verbal and written. Thinking skills which include reasoning and logic, decision-making and problem solving, will also be extremely important. And thirdly, members of our future working force must have interpersonal skills and personal qualities that enable them to lead, serve, negotiate, manage, teach, and work well with people from culturally diverse backgrounds.

A cousin of mine who had been to Taiwan returned to tell me that 15% of that country's gross national product is committed to education. The Republic of China as it is officially named, is the world's twelfth largest economy and generates $70-80 billion in foreign currency reserves annually. Mathematics has never been my strong suit, but you can easily calculate the dollar amount that it represents.

Meanwhile in state after state in the U.S.A., education budgets are being slashed at a time when our country can least afford it. A recent print ad published by the Chrysler Corporation says it well. Under a picture of two school-age children, the copy reads, "If they fail in the 20th century, America will fail in the 21st."

In contrast, for millennia of Chinese history, a system of stringent national examinations were established to recruit and capitalize on the country's best minds. Only the country's top achievers could attain civil positions which with them carried status and its privileges.

Here's just a sampling of some old Asian sayings on the subject of education:

- A nation's treasure....scholars.

- The little learned man is useful to the state, what use is the great big blockhead?

- Gold has its price, learning is beyond price

- Learn to handle a writing brush....and you'll never handle a begging bowl

- Learning is weightless...treasure you always carry easily

- Son without learning, you have raised an ass.

- Daughter without learning, you have raised a pig.

You get the picture. This emphasis on education meant a poor farmer's son or that of a noble could attain a high and respectable position that paid well by being a dedicated scholar. It also meant that if a person was not born into comfortable circumstances, through education, one could study one's way up the social ladder. Families would lighten the student's domestic obligations to allow him to study. And the rulers of China surrounded themselves with the most highly educated in the kingdom.

The proof is in the pudding so to speak. China is the oldest continuous civilization in the world and in its prime produced a wealth of inventions and discoveries that impact our lives today. Robert Temple's ***The Genius of China: 3,000 Years of Science, Discovery, and Invention*** details an impressive array of examples.

This same accent on education spread to other doctrines of Confucian philosophy that focused on duty, virtue, modesty, frugality, public service, and ceremony. Duty was especially important, as it was directed towards one's family first, and each member brought pride or disgrace to his family accordingly. The pressure, therefore, was on every student to achieve academically to bring honor to the family name. A native son who had passed his examinations could therefore contribute not only prestige to his village, but also financial resources to improve its lot. Those who were educated were highly respected and admired.

Through the centuries, the examination system has survived until today in many Asian countries, such as Taiwan, Hong Kong, and Japan. Compared to the United States, the opportunities for higher education, and consequently, for employment are limited because the countries are much smaller than ours. Therefore, it is imperative that the universities screen out and accept only the creme de la creme of the nation's best.

Korea, for example, has the highest number of Ph.D.'s in the world, but only one third of the graduating high school students can be accommodated in the country's institutions of higher learning. That percentage will increase to 40% in the next decade. Various college guides here in the United States average about two inches in thickness, the information printed in 2-point type, and according to a **Time** magazine cover story (April 13, 1992), lists "156 universities, 1,953 four-year colleges, 1,378 two-year colleges and technical schools....employing 793,000 faculty members." In contrast, most Asian countries have fewer than a dozen institutions of higher learning each.

Each year the national examinations are a spring rite which generates much anxiety for high school seniors and their families. Unlike our SATs and ACTs, everybody takes them, although for many, preparations for this crucial exam would have been going on since tutoring began in kindergarten. This tradition is taken very seriously and doing well can make or break one's future.

It is not uncommon for wives of Japanese corporate executives who have been assigned to the United States to refuse to move here for fear that their offspring will get too far behind and will be unable to catch up. In Asian country after country it was always considered the responsibility of the parents to provide an education for their offspring, especially for males. Parents generally did not feel their responsibility was completed until this had been achieved.

A woman I know is a typical example. She married while a junior in college, but her father asked that her diploma for her bachelor of arts degree from USC be issued with her maiden name. A small request to be sure, but highly symbolic of the closure of her father's responsibility.

If a student achieves high marks, (s)he is assured a spot at one of the few universities in each country, thus leading to a degree, possibly attendance at a foreign university (e.g. in the United

States), and practically guaranteed a job with a major company. This equates to a secure future for oneself and eventually, one's family.

It is no wonder, then that there is a predominance of Asian Pacific students in our universities for only the very best have earned the right to study in the United States. Four hundred seven thousand, five hundred thirty students from 193 countries came to study in America in 1991; 39,600 from China and 36,610 from Japan alone. They come already accustomed to studying hard and typically aim for admission to the best that American education has to offer, often the Ivy league institutions on the East Coast and the top-ranked universities on the West.

In 1990, Asians for the first time outnumbered non-Asians among the incoming freshman at UCLA, 37% v.s. 33%. A **Los Angeles Times** article dated April 5, 1992, reports: "In 1990, 61.5% of all Asian American high school students are eligible for Cal State, compared to 38.2% of Anglo students, 18.6% of African-Americans and 17.3% of Latinos.

"A whopping 40.4% of Asian American students were eligible for UC, compared to 20.5% for Anglos, 7.5% for African-Americans and 6.8% for Latinos".

Among American Asians, those of Filipino ancestry have the largest families, numbering 3.47 members; those of Asian Indian descent have the smallest families, 2.37 members, compared to the 3.34 members in the non-Hispanic white family.

Among the foreign-born, the Vietnamese have the largest families, numbering 4.88 , while the Japanese have the smallest at 3.01 members, compared to 2.94 for non-Hispanic whites.

The **Chinese Consumer Yellow Pages and Business Guide and Business Guide** devotes fifteen pages before its advertised listings to information on the SATs as well as a roster of the top 25 American universities, and a comprehensive listing in minuscule type of the 50 most highly-ranked American colleges and universities in 68 categories.

I would like to offer a layperson's observation as to why so many Asia-educated immigrant children do so well in school, even though no or limited English may be spoken in their homes. The first reason is that education is a family affair, involving everyone from the parents who oversee homework assignments to the youngest offspring who are assisted by older siblings. The pressure on Asian youngsters is tremendous to achieve academically and much has been written on the success of immigrant children.

As for doing well in mathematics and the sciences, Asian children seem to be way ahead of those in other groups. One explanation may be that in these disciplines, there is less emphasis on English language skills in which most Asian immigrant children are weak. Another reason I would like to suggest is that much of the education in Asia is based on rote memory just as theories and formulas are. Asian languages, unlike English, are not based on combining the twenty-six letters of an alphabet, but rather pictographs and symbols, necessitating memorization of thousands of individual words and characters.

The February 1992 issue of **Scientific American** gives a detailed report on research done of the academic success of Southeast Asian children. Its main point was that family support was overwhelmingly the determining factor in the success of these youngsters, many of whom spoke no English when they entered the schools here in the United States. Parents and older siblings contributed time and financial resources, e.g., through tutoring, to give the children the critical leg-up to get ahead.

What subjects are being taught overseas? A random sampling of high school transcripts from several Asian countries gives us an idea:

Indonesia

Religious Study

Geography

Moral Education

Economics/Accounting

History of the Nation Struggle

Sociology and Anthropology

Indonesian Language Study

Political Science

Mathematics

Foreign Language

Iran

Persian Reading and Grammar

Arabic

Ecology Based on Civics

Religions and Morals

English Reading and Conversation

Mathematics

Physics and Chemistry and Lab

Tools Technology

Mass Media

Discipline

Economics

Sociology

Statistics

Japan

Japanese

Social Studies

Japanese History

Mathematics

Science

Physical Education

Japan (continued)

Health Education

Japanese Calligraphy

English

General Home Economics

Clothing

General Business

Bookkeeping

Abacus Calculation

Computer Programming

Office Education

Business Law

Korea

National Ethics

Korean

Politics and Economics

Korean Geography

Mathematics

Chemistry

Biology

Physical Training

Military Training

Music

Art

Chinese Writing

English

French

Peoples Republic of China

Politics

Chinese

English

Mathematics

Peoples Republic of China (continued)

Physics

Chemistry

Physical Training

Republic of China (Taiwan)

Civics

Chinese

English

Business English

Mathematics

Bookkeeping

Introduction to Commerce

Abacus Skills

Music

Economics

Typewriting (English)

Accounting

Translation

English Composition

Banking and Money

Enterprise Management

Marketing

English Shorthand

Physical Education

Military Training

Thailand

Thai

Social Studies

Health Education

Biology

General Business

Consumer Economics

Thailand (continued)

English

Mathematics

Contemporary Events

Speech

Art Appreciation

East Asian in Contemporary World

Thai Typing

Bookkeeping

Economic Geography

Historical Background of Thai Literature

Introduction to Urbanism

Introduction to Library Study

The weakest links in Asian education I believe are in creativity, critical thinking skills and problem-solving, which are commonly included in the interdisciplinary curricula found here in the States. An educated citizenry may also have been viewed as dangerous, for they could think for themselves; and thousands of years of Asian rulers on the continent maintained their control, relying heavily on the fact that the masses were simple, uneducated farm folks.

Asian students who immigrate to this country with their families have the best of both educational worlds. They have family support academically, rigorous study habits instilled at an early age, and they have an opportunity to be more creative and innovative in their thinking in the American system. Moreover, their homes are those in which education is highly prized. Their parents want very much for their offspring to enjoy a better life than they.

CHAPTER FIVE

MONEY MATTERS

Confucian ethics pervade into money matters and the way Asians generally view them. Frugality was taught as a virtue and thriftiness was the norm. Today the average Japanese family saves 22-25% of its income compared to the 2-3% of income saved by Americans (more recently this figure has risen to 6% during the recession). In Taiwan, the savings rate is said to be an astounding 70%!

Asians in the United States generally have more workers per household (thus explaining the higher income) but individually earn 20% less than white Americans, and aspire to own their own business as opposed to being employed.

Education, the work ethic, frugality, respect for group authority, obligation and duty to the family, especially elders and parents - these are the elements that combine in a powerful mix which propel Asian countries to the top of the global marketplace. Taiwan, Singapore, South Korea, and Hong Kong, nicknamed the "Four Little Dragons/Tigers," are following the example of economic powerhouse Japan. Thailand, Indonesia, Malaysia, and the Philippines are not far behind.

Some of us are old enough to remember when the words "Made in Japan" or "Made in Taiwan" meant merchandise that was either copied or shoddily-made, but no more. These little dragons now lead the world in their manufacture of ships, toys, apparel, shoes, automobiles, textiles, and electronics.

Although many Asian banks have sprung up in metropolitan areas in the United States, there are still a large number of Asian immigrants who do not put their money into them. Being able to pay for something in cash is a matter of pride, and to buy on credit was and is a cause for loss of face.

The vice president at one of the oldest Chinese-American banks in California told me that it took a major marketing effort to persuade potential customers to buy on credit. The reason was the Chinese custom of paying off all debts before the lunar new year began. People in Chinese communities had difficulty changing their customary thinking about holding a debt over into the new year. Buying on credit is obviously a learned behavior and necessitated a major cultural shift in their cultural mindset.

In my home I was raised, as many Asians are, to pay for things with cash. If I didn't have the money, I did without. I learned at an early age that if I saved money, I could afford to buy something I needed or wanted when I desired. Unlike here in the United States, most people in Asia carry cash to pay for the their goods and services. It is ironic to observe that today, many Asians who view their "gold cards" as status symbols when in reality it represents a deferment in payment. But concern for personal safety and a rising crime rate in some Asian countries is a very practical reason why carrying credit cards instead of cash has gained popularity.

One of the questions that invariably comes up during my seminars is, "Who holds the purse strings in a family, the husband or the wife?" There are as many answers as there are families, so there are no hard and fast rules. Many Asian men hand over their paychecks and their wives handle all the family finances as well as all aspects of their children's education.

Or as one fellow said, "I have three sets of books: one that I show the IRS, one that I show my accountant, and one that I show my wife." In family-owned businesses, the accounting is always done by a close relative who can be relied upon to be discreet and maintain confidentiality. By doing this, the true earnings or worth of a company is generally not public knowledge. Moreover, modesty has also been viewed as a virtue in Asian cultures so it serves businesses well when they do not wish to disclose such private matters as their finances.

Another topic that departs from American custom regards the giving of money to people for their services. Among my clients who range from the City of Monterey Park Fire Department to retail businesses to major developers, this subject almost invariably comes up and is discussed at length. There are very strict laws regarding the acceptance of material and monetary gifts as well as favors and preferential treatment in most companies in the United States. To do so is considered graft. On the other hand, "payola" in many Asian (and non-Asian countries in the world) is the lubricant that keeps societies and governments moving. In the past several decades, however, there has been a concerted effort in countries such as Taiwan and Hong Kong to combat graft. But thousands of years of tradition and practice make it difficult to eliminate totally.

Gifts and favors are perceived very differently than in this country where they are considered as outright bribes. But gift-giving in a country such as Japan is a national tradition and a major business. In other Asian countries, they <u>ensure</u> prompt or speedy service, rather than being a <u>reward</u> for exceptional service.

For example, if you live in an area where the community services are limited, such as in a small town or village, each year you may invite the chief of the fire or police department for dinner several times in celebration of festivals, holidays, or family events. Should your house catch on fire or be robbed at the same time as another person, hopefully the chief, remembering all those delicious meals you hosted, would be more inclined to respond first to <u>your</u> house.

Those of you who have visited Las Vegas and attended a dinner show for any popular performer know exactly what I am talking about. A folded bill slipped into the hand of the captain as you follow him in the dark ensures a good seat close to the stage.

"She works hard for her money," goes a Donna Summer hit from several years ago. For Asian families who have scrimped and saved to afford pulling up their roots and transplanting themselves and their families here, this is even more so. Just like every other immigrant group that has come to the United States, Asians have come to take advantage of the vast opportunities in America and to seek a better life for employment openings are very limited in Asia. There is a disproportionate number of applicants for the few jobs available. For years, I have heard the saying, "If you are willing to work, you will never starve in America."

The Marketplace

For people who treasure knowledge and learning, the entire world of commerce has been viewed very seriously for centuries.

Since the 5th century B.C. Chinese scholars have been studying and applying the 36 stratagems of war to commerce and business. Written by Sun Wu, the thirteen chapters of **The Art of War** have been hailed as a classic treatise for not only military applications, but to business leadership, administration and productivity as well. The four sections focus on a) knowing oneself as well as the enemy (competition) b) making oneself invincible and well organized c) being ingenious creative/resourceful to stay ahead of the competition d) the essential qualities to be a good leader.

Evelyn Lip's **Notes on Things Chinese** gives a sampling of some of these stratagems:

- Stop your competitors from getting near or catching up with you.
- Transfer a competitor or get him out of the way.
- Use others to eliminate your enemies.
- Expose an opponent's plot.
- Distract the attention of your enemies.
- Wait for your opponent to act first.

The marketplace is a battleground.
-Chinese proverb

- Wait for an opportunity or create one.

- Set an example.

- Avoid embarrassing situations.

- Get something for nothing.

- Use your resources.

- Hide your feelings.

- Be aggressive.

- Get down to the source of the problem.

- Point out one mistake to expose others.

- Be patient.

- Take calculated risks.

- Pretend to be stupid.

- Set an example.

- Strike.

- Use the unusual to be ahead.

As many of the most affluent in Asian countries were ethnic Chinese, it is not surprising that their business acumen was legendary. In some countries, this group was envied and resented, resulting in many local regulations and laws being enacted to suppress their entrepreneurial endeavors. Some were the victims of violence.

The Japanese also have studied military strategy for centuries (see Thomas Cleary and Miyamoto Musashi's publications listed in the bibliography at the back of this book) and have been applying the principles to business and business management. Just recently, some of these books are showing up on the business section shelves of major bookstore chains here in the States.

Not every Asian businessman or woman is a scholar and studies the *The Art of War* in order to do business with American and European companies. But having learned the Japanese or Chinese classics as a part of their literature requirements in school, many have an advantage. Most, however, learn how to manage a business merely by being a part of a family that owned one. But then there are those who had to learn the ropes on their own. Their education in negotiating skills may have started at the city marketplace when they had been entrusted with some money to buy vegetables for the evening meal.

Here in America we are at a disadvantage because negotiating is not a part of our general education while our Asian counterparts may have been bargaining since they were children! After all, most Asian countries have agrarian roots which produced a "market mentality," as well as skills in haggling and bartering. More than 2,500 years ago, Central Asia was the center of commerce and exchange of technology, consumer goods, culture, and religion. When my family moved from Wellington, New Zealand to Taipei, Taiwan, haggling was one of the skills that I had to learn. With many cousins tutoring me, I soon developed the knack. If you have ever been approached by ten street peddlers simultaneously on the beach at Acapulco or shopped in the garment districts of New York or Los Angeles, or at a flea market in any other part of the country, you have probably had some practice in this area.

For those of you who have not had this cultural experience, I would like to share some basic, unwritten rules:

1.   Only negotiate if you are serious about buying.
2.   Offer half of the asking price and work up until a price is agreed on.
3.   Maintain the spirit by keeping your humor and temper.

Imagine that you are walking down "Women's Street" in Hong Kong. It is a five-block-long stretch of Kowloon that is crowded with peddlers who sell their wares from wheeled booths, practically hiding the many storefronts behind. Some of the merchandise you see is similar and most of the peddlers are calling out to you as you walk by. Finally you decide that you want to purchase a shirt that you have seen in several of the stalls and you stop at one.

Your exchange with the peddler might go something like this:

"How much is that shirt?" you ask, pointing to the shirt of your choice.

"Eighty dollars," comes the answer.

Doing quick calculations in your head, you realized that with the one-to-seven-dollar exchange rate, you could never get this shirt at Nordstrom's Rack back home on for this price.

"That's too much," you comment, hoping that your delight in the low price isn't showing, "forty dollars."

"Ha, ha," the peddler laughs, "you can't get this shirt anywhere else for under this price."

Silly you, you think, and turn around to walk to the next stall, "Thank you."

The peddler sees his customer and profit literally walking away, "Seventy dollars," he calls out, waving you back.

You smile a little deviously and stop where you are. "Fifty dollars," you say, turning back to him.

"I have to feed my wife and six children" he says plaintively, "how about sixty-five?"

"Fifty five," you counter, turning away again.

"Sixty three."

"Sixty."

"Okay, okay," he agrees.

When you started the bargaining, you knew darn well that you were not going to pay the full price. Likewise, the peddler knew he wouldn't get the eighty dollars, but he had to try anyway, knowing there was a slim chance that you were a first-time tourist who would pay the asking price or a softie who would feel just awful even bargaining at all when the price was already so low. He also knew that he wasn't going to sell the shirt for what you offered. Most importantly, both of you wanted a transaction to take place, so you each gave and took a little until you reached an accord. Finally, a win-win situation evolve: you got the shirt and he made a sale to feed his family.

Of course, not all international negotiations are as simple as haggling in the alleys of Hong Kong. In the creating of multi-million dollar trans-Pacific contracts, there is an entirely new intercultural dimension which is absent from deal-making between American companies.

Several books are available on how to do business in specific Asian countries. ***Getting Your Yen's Worth, How to Negotiate with Japan, Inc.*** by Robert T. Moran is one of them. Also available are: ***International Negotiating, a Cross Cultural Perspective*** by Glen Fisher; ***National Negotiating Styles*** edited by Hans Binnendijk, ***World-Class Negotiating*** by Donald and Rebecca Hendon; Philip Harris and Robert Moran devote fifteen pages to the general topic of cross-cultural negotiating in ***Managing Cultural Differences*** and ***Going International*** by Lennie Copeland and Lewis Griggs. Some guidelines from the Copeland/Griggs book suggest:

1. Making sure that what you are negotiating is negotiable.
2. Defining what "winning" the negotiations means to you.
3. Being ambitious, but setting a realistic walk-away.
4. Getting the facts and finding out what is important to the other side.
5. Having a strategy for each culture and each phase and deciding how to position your proposal (cooperative: win/win or competitive: win/lose); setting your opening offers and planning to control your concessions.
6. Sending a winning team and <u>not</u> going alone; leaving your attorneys and accountants out of the negotiating team.

Going International © 1985, by Lennie Copeland and Lewis Griggs. A Plume ® Book. Reprinted by permission of the authors.

Even in Roger Axtell's ***Do's and Taboos of Hosting International Visitors***, the author gives a list of thirteen mistakes that American negotiators make:

- Ignoring the etiquette of the culture across the table.
- Not negotiating face-to-face.
- Ignoring the importance of rank.
- Jumping right into business without a period of socializing.
- Assuming American ways are the only ways to do business.
- Lacking patience.
- Assuming "yes" means "I agree" when it could very likely mean "Yes, I hear you."

- When hitting a roadblock, failing to retrace steps and examining, if perhaps, one misunderstood word or phrase was the cause.
- Failing to review, affirm, confirm key points.
- Assuming an interpreter is always 100 percent accurate.
- Failing to have the authority to make decisions on the spot.
- Assuming that, as in America, all cultures view a final agreement as fixed in cement.

Do's and Taboos of Hosting International Visitors Copyright © 1990, by Roger E. Axtell, John Wiley & Sons. Reprinted by permission of John Wiley & Sons, Inc.

Knowing that negotiating is an integral part of the Asian way of doing business, it pays to include some flexibility in pricing your product. Always keeping your profit margin in mind and build in some "negotiation space," because many Asians will never view the last price quoted or printed as the one they will pay for something.

For example, if you are a retailer with a showroom full of furniture and accessories, you may rethink your big "40-70% off" sign painted on the window, or if you are a developer, the "Homes priced between $150,000 to $250,000" clause on the sales brochure.

What do those signs really mean to a potential consumer anyway, Asian or non-Asian? Are some items 40% off and other 70% off? Why is there a difference for different pieces or different models? Some people would look at the prices and may think that they can negotiate to get a cheaper price on the $150,000 home. And haggle they will, perhaps wearing you down, to show their business acumen.

Spending Money

On what do Asians and Asian Americans spend their money? They enjoy life and pursue the American dream!

According to figures supplied by Muse, Cordero, Chen, Asian purchasing power is worth $225 billion annually and a recent report in the <u>Chinese Daily News</u> gave insight into their spending habits. They enjoy traveling, entertainment, exercise, sports, music and concerts, photography, reading, dining out, gambling, and owning their own homes.

With their earning power the highest of all groups, many can well afford spending their discretionary income on luxury items such as signature clothing, imported automobiles, and expensive liquor. It is no wonder then that airlines with Pacific routes, distributors of fine cognacs and brandies, and other up-scale businesses are reaching out to the Asian and Asian American population throughout the country.

Deloitte Touche published its findings on the San Francisco Bay area Asian consumers in March, 1990. 500 households were surveyed and the results are enough to make any marketer take notice.

BAY AREA CONSUMERS

	Asians	General Population
Single	47%	31%
Student	22.4%	10.7%
College degree	28.9%	18.5%
Professional or managerial job	33.7%	32%
Males	37.6%	36.2%
Females	29.3%	29.3%
Income $40K+	40%	27%
Live with family or parents	28.1%	13.6%
Speak other than English at home	25.7%	2.6%
Average age (in years)	33.4%	40.8%

In other research conducted by KSCI, Los Angeles, consumer habits of the Southern California Chinese, Vietnamese, Korean, and Japanese were studied.

KSCI SOUTHERN CALIFORNIA ASIAN CONSUMER SURVEY

GROUP	Attended college	Earnings over $30,000	Lived in U.S. all their lives	Lived in U.S. less than 10 years	Have relatives immigrating to U.S. in 1990-1995	Native language preferred	Own home	Rent home	Own business	Own life insurance	Teach native language to children	Air travel annually	International travel/carrier
Chinese	51%	NA	5%	58%	28%	89%	60%	NA	18%	45%	NA	66%	1 China Airlines 46% 2 Singapore 3 American
Japanese	70%	60%	62%	16%	8%	28%	74%	13%	16%	75%	61%	NA	41%
Korean	70%	60%	1%	42%	25%	66%	57%	35%	42%	50%	94%	NA	NA
Vietnamese	NA	19%	0%	66%	29%	86%	33%	NA	NA	NA	NA	NA	NA

GROUP	Automobile	Amusement	Bank	Coffee	Computer (own PC)	Department Store	Detergent	Gasoline	Milk	Shampoo	Toothpaste	Travel Destination Las Vegas & Reno (1 or both in 2 years)	VCR ownership
Chinese	1 Toyota 2 Honda 3 Ford	77% to Disney-land	1 Bank of America 2 Cathay Pacific	NA	38%	Broadway	Tide	Union 76	NA	1 Head & Shoulders 2 Prell	Colgate	72%	80%
Japanese	1 Toyota 2 Nissan	66% to Disney-land	1 B of A 2 California Bank	1 Yuban 2 Folgers	NA	1 Nordstroms 2 Bullocks	NA	Union 76	Lowfat	NA	NA	86% (Averaged 3.5 times/year)	NA
Korean	1. Toyota 2 Chevrolet	82% to Disney-land	1 B of A 2 Korean Bank	1 Taster's Choice 2 Folgers	NA	Broadway	NA	Union 76	Whole	NA	NA	75%	NA
Vietnamese	1 Toyota 2 Nissan 3 Honda	70% to Disney-land	1 B of A, 2 Security Pacific	NA	23%	1 K Mart 2 May Co.	Tide	1 ARCO 2 Shell	NA	NA	Colgate	37%	63%

The Los Angeles-based <u>Korea Times</u>' study published a 127-page report on Korean-American consumers. 49.8% of Koreans own homes and two-thirds of them purchase a house within ten years of immigration. The median price of a Korean-owned home was $280,000 and 42.8% are worth $300,000 or more. 8.8% are valued at half a million (1989) dollars. More than half make those home purchases through Korean realtors and about 40% through non-Korean.

In Orange County, California, Data Information Systems recently revealed a fascinating study. In 1991, 456 homes averaging $200,000 in value were sold to buyers whose last name was Nguyen; 254 homes averaging $275,571 in price were sold to buyers with the surname Lee, 162 to those with the name Kim; 114 to the Vus; 112 to the Phams; 110 to the Trans, and 106 to the Buis. Number three on the list was those with the surname of Smith who bought 218 homes, averaging $209, 227.

Sources of money can be elusive, as anyone who works for a title company or a lending institution can attest. Many Asians are reluctant to reveal the sources of their income and remain secretive about their finances. For some, having to borrow from parents and relatives to subsidize or support them while getting started here in the States represents a major loss of face. Others who do not wish to disclose confidential information may be moonlighting or just want to keep the sources of their financial support private. Still, a third segment may be sensitive to personal safety and not wish to flaunt their wealth, although there are many who do.

When new immigrants move here from Asia, a great number of them have no credit history and therefore are viewed as a poor credit risk by the mainstream banks. Moreover, they do not understand the American banking system or have limited English proficiency with which to conduct their business transactions. They may also be seeking a banking institution that understands their culture, hence the proliferation of Asian-owned banks in the United States in the past thirty years. These financial institutions fill the niche that mainstream American banks left, providing services that were extremely responsive to their clients' personal and commercial banking needs.

In addition to Asian-owned banks with multi-lingual tellers and loan officers, there exists another system through which cash or credit can be found. Loosely translated, these "loan clubs" are called a <u>hui</u> (literally "association" or "meeting") in Chinese and Vietnamese; a <u>kye</u> in Korean, and <u>ko</u> in Japanese. (Also known as a <u>tanda</u> to Mexicans and <u>su-su</u> to West Indians.)

Women operate many of these loan clubs as they often control the finances in Asian families, as the men are thought to be too tempted by outside distractions to be trusted with money!

The concept is a simple one, based on trust, honesty, family honor, and need, among other things. A group of people, numbering between four to twenty people who are often strangers to each other, are organized by a central person. Members contribute money to a pool for the use of those who are in the greatest need---to pay for a wedding, to start a new business, to provide medical treatment for an ailing parent. While the agreement regarding interest and payback may vary from club to club, the main point is that those who participate can be loaned a much greater sum that what they put in. Many Asians also utilize the group for savings, much as how one would use a credit union. A 1987 survey conducted by a UCLA sociologist among 110 Los Angeles Koreans in the garment industry found that 18.1% of respondents obtained their start-up capital in this fashion and 77.3% said that at least one person in their household used a kye for either savings or borrowing.

I would like to offer one final word about how many Asians view money in general. In contrast to the American view of "Time is money," it is important to remember that relationships are invariably valued over time or money. Friendships and consideration of the other partner's face may take precedence over profit.

As relationships take many years and much participation between the parties to develop, trust and respect represent the cement in the foundation. It is not unheard of for families to have close ties with each other for many generations, unlike in the States where mobility and family breakups unravel the threads of relationships before they can ever be woven.

The bottom line therefore becomes secondary or low priority to how a potential partner's "heart", or sincerity, is perceived. Is he of good character? Can he be trusted? If this is such a good deal that he wants me to joint venture with him, how come he's not willing to put in 51% of his own money? Why has he asked me to foot the bulk of the investment while he only invests a measly 10 or 15%? Is the prospective partner one who is simpatico? Does he really care about me, or is he out to make the quick buck or take advantage of me?

In negotiations, what do the parties really want? In our quest to reach the bottom line, we are often totally off the mark. I am reminded of a story I heard about a salesperson who worked very hard to acquire a piece of property for his client to build a shopping center. For many months negotiations went back and forth, creating a great deal of frustration and anxiety for the salesperson who had spent a good part of a year trying to buy the property and whose income was dependent on making the sale. The owners of the property were an elderly couple whose family had lived in the old house at the site for many years and who had raised several children there. No matter how much money was offered, it was turned down. The salesperson used his best selling techniques and arguments that had been successful in the past, both aggressive and subtle, to no avail. At the final meeting, he threw his hands up in resignation and told the owner that he was giving up and that he would agree to whatever the man wanted for the property. To his total amazement, the owner told him the reason why he and his wife didn't want to sell. To them the site represented their history and happiness. If they sold it, the history of the family would be reduced to concrete and asphalt, thereby obliterating the presence and memories of the many generations of his family that had lived in the community.

It was only then that the salesperson realized in an instant what the man's point was...a cherished family home that had been the site of so many happy memories could not be reduced to the terms of cold, hard cash. The solution was actually a simple one and he immediately offered it...to name the shopping center after the family so they would not be forgotten. The owner picked up the telephone right away and called his wife who immediately agreed to the sale.

CHAPTER SIX

THE LANGUAGE OF MARKETING

While we are on the subject of homebuying and property, I would like to use an illustration of the cultural minefield you may encounter if you fail to look at your product or merchandise from the viewpoint of another person's culture.

Imagine this scene at a new housing development. Blue and white banners beckoned in the Saturday afternoon breeze, marking the boundaries of the new subdivision. The brick path leading to the sales office was bordered with white chrysanthemums, gold shasta daisies, and electric blue pansies.

"Fireplaces, cathedral ceilings, clerestory windows, custom radius walls, curving staircases, wide sliding glass doors, cheery breakfast nooks overlooking avocado and lemon trees" and the proximity of the development to the local hospital as well as other community services were featured in an attractive brochure.

And who could possibly resist the beautifully decorated model homes on display? Model A with its country look, decorated in French blue with the gentle scent of potpourri throughout the house; traditional Model B with its rich dark wood mouldings and hunting scenes in gilded frames gracing the walls; or Model C reflecting the current Southwestern trends, with the painted wooden snake, samples of historic barb wire on the family room walls, sun-bleached steer's skull, and cactus in the living room.

Stop! Take a look again at the project again, this time through culturally-colored glasses, those of that Asian couple just getting out of their Mercedes sedan. To them the blue and white flags are suggestive of a funeral procession; as do the gold, white, and blue flowers, the colors of mourning. All those dried flowers and petal decorating the interior of Model A almost guarantee that their love life will suffer; that wreath of dried roses and baby's breath above the master bed does not bode well at all.

The "cathedral ceiling" touted in the brochure puzzles them because they cannot understand what the ceiling of a church is doing inside a home. Mrs. Chang sighs as she asks her husband for the meaning of the word "nook" and "clerestory" as she has not brought her bi-lingual dictionary with her. Although he has several degrees in engineering, he is stumped over the description of "custom radius walls." Could that mean that he can actually choose the exact curvature of the corner?

And that curving staircase facing the front door in Model B is bad news. Mr. Chang, who preparing to start a new business, sees his good fortune go rolling right out as it does in Model A with its French doors lining up with the front entrance across the living room.

And what is that unusual fruit called the avocado growing next to the lemon tree in the backyard? Sour fruit. Those paintings of dead ducks and quail next to the wine and fruit of Model B dismay Mrs. Chang. The morbidity of those and the fox hunting scenes make her feel uncomfortable as she hurries down the hall, averting her eyes.

The Changs agree that the color scheme in Model C is pleasing, but not the snake, plastic cactus plant, and especially the sun-whitened skull with the hollow eye sockets. Shaking their heads, they get into their car and drive out of the parking lot, commenting as they leave that they had just wasted their time.

The scenario I have just described is merely an example of looking at a product from another cultural point of view. It is not to say that every perspective customer or client of Asian descent thinks like the two fictional characters. I only use this story to raise your awareness of some of the factors that could further impact your sales and marketing decisions. Usually Asian-owned businesses have sprung up around neighborhood ethnic enclaves, and it is safe to say that you would be hard-pressed to match the prices that they offer. The ***Chinese Yellow Pages and Business Guide*** in the Los Angeles area, mentioned earlier in this book, for example, contains almost 1,500 pages and many non-Asian-owned businesses that do advertise in it.

Does this mean that it is hopeless for you to try to crack the Asian market? NO! All you need is one happy customer or client and you will have discovered the most important secret of reaching this group: <u>word of mouth.</u> As I am fond of saying in my seminars, you can spend a million dollars on your Asian marketing effort, but it would not be as effective as one of your customers picking up the telephone and telling it through the grapevine. This has been confirmed over and over again from the many vice presidents and directors of sales and marketing who are my clients.

Think about it this way, when you first moved into a new neighborhood after you got the job or earned your degree, you didn't know where anything was - where to find a good barber or beauty salon, or a mechanic to service your car. Over a period of time, you met your neighbors and co-workers as well as made friends through your church or temple, business, or local civic and service organizations that you joined. In a pinch when your washing machine or refrigerator gave out, you might have had to consult the yellow pages, but more likely than not you probably patronized the businesses that were referred to you by colleagues, friends, and neighbors whose judgment you trusted.

The same applies to your Asian market, but even more so. Word-of-mouth marketing is the most cost-effective and productive method of getting the word out into Asian communities. Asian and Asian American families are networks within themselves and you can use them to your advantage By using the knowledge you gained in Chapter Four, you can now transfer it to tap into the communities you want to reach.

You can also use print or electronic media. I strongly urge you to start immediately to set aside resources for this method. During down times such as a recession and traditionally slow seasonal periods, go through your database of past Asian clients and customers. Use these times to build up your referral network.

Call up your past successful closures, ask how they are doing or how they are enjoying the use of the new purchase they made from you. Furthermore, ask them if they know of any friends or family members who need the same item, and may you call those folks, using their names as referrals? Thank them very much for their time and referrals and suggest they call you if there is anything you can do for them. Make a note on your calendar to send them a holiday greeting card or one for their birthday, such as that which I get each year from my State Farm Insurance friend who just happens to be a Chinese from Malaysia.

But don't forget.the grapevine works both ways. Just as the news travels about the great deal they got at your store, so does any broken promises, forgotten followup, unreturned messages, or neglect. You and your company have to earn the trust and respect to be the topic on the network.

The customer creed I read on a client's wall says it all:

-   A customer is the most important person ever to this company

-   A customer is not dependent on us, we are dependent on them

-   A customer is not an interruption of our work, they are the purpose of it

-   We are not doing a favor by serving them, they are doing us a favor by giving us the opportunity to do so

-   A customer is not someone to argue or match wits with, nobody ever won an argument with a customer

-   A customer is a person who brings their wants, it is our job to handle those wants profitably for them and for ourselves

Relationships and relationship-building are the most important threads in the fabric of Asian societies. This tradition does not end when those of Asian ancestry move to the United States. In many cases, it becomes even more important to those who come here because they have pulled up their roots, transplanted to a new land and need to surround themselves with things that are familiar to help them feel secure and comfortable. Traditions, customs, and languages are among those.

Speaking of comfort, another question that I am asked often is whether a business should hire Asian sales staff. Yes and no. Yes, if the Asian sales person is one who can connect with and sell to your target public. No, if he or she cannot.

"Do Asians prefer to buy from someone who speaks their language and do they patronize only Asian businesses?" is one of the most often-asked questions at my seminars. Some do and some don't. If your target public is concentrated in an area heavily populated by many other Asians, it may indicate that they may be newer immigrants who have the need to feel more secure being around others like themselves. There is a certain comfort level in a shared culture.

If your clients are in an area with many Southeast Asians, you would be most successful hiring a person who is knowledgeable, with a "soft touch." If you have many potential customers who are accustomed to the fast-paced, energetic, fast-talking Hong Kong style, you need a sales person who is the same way. Those of you in sales have heard it before: you are most effective "mirroring" your customer.

To hear the message through heavy accents, garbled syntax, and mumbled mispronunciation is a valuable gift. The constantly talking salesperson is usually also one who lacks patience and caring, and most importantly, the ability to listen, all of which matter to an Asian client. A person who is patient and who can empathize and help a non-native English speaker articulate his wants and needs clearly is a gem. Hire him or her immediately.

I would like to interject a short story about a student of mine who went away on a trip one weekend, returning to share the experience with her classmates on Monday morning. She and her family had entered a coffee shop for breakfast and the waitress came to ask for her order.

"How do you want your eggs?" she was asked.

Poor kid. Imagine the many different ways a person can have an egg-prepared: scrambled, over-easy, soft, hard, or medium boiled, and sunnyside up.

My student pondered the question a minute and then told the waitress.

"I want eggs like two suns."

When her order came, she was ecstatic. She got what she wanted -two eggs sunnyside up.

The point is that those who do not have a good command of English struggle very hard to be understood and suffer a great deal of frustration when their listeners second guess them, complete their sentences, and misinterpret what they are trying to communicate.

Many Asians (and non-Asians, come to think about it) abhor the aggressive, pushy salesperson who talks speedily and constantly. It is wiser for you to hire someone who sincerely likes people, is patient, and can really listen well.   Many people who love to talk rarely know how to listen or hear what others have to say. If your Asian customers have little or limited-English-speaking experience or proficiency, this one skill is the most crucial in choosing your sales staff.

Patience has its rewards when you take time to listen carefully. Those who learn English as their second, third, fourth or fifth language find it difficult and frustrating not knowing how to express themselves as well as they would like. Let's face it, our language is a crazy quilt of all our immigrant tongues; each square contributing to its richness and variety. But those same thousand of words cause confusion and misunderstanding.

We Americans talk too quickly, are sloppy in our pronunciation and use too many figurative expressions as well as the vernacular. We always need to keep in mind that Asians who have come to our country did not learn English as their first language. Their first exposure to it was at the junior high school level and they may read and write it better than they speak it. If you put yourself into their shoes, you can better appreciate the difficulties they experience. Imagine yourself doing business with the French, German, or Spanish you learned in high school. Your mind has to make translations in your head before you can make the words come out of your mouth!

The following poem by an anonymous author gives you an idea of how we take our American English language for granted:

Our Strange Language

We'll begin with a box and the plural is boxes
But the plural of ox is oxen, not oxes
Then one fowl is a goose but two are called geese
Yet the plural of moose should never be meese

You find a lone mouse or a whole set of mice,
Yet the plural of house is houses, not hice.
If the plural of man is always called men,
Why shouldn't the plural of pan be called pen?

If I speak of food and you show me your feet,
And I give you a boot, would a pair be called beet?
If one is a tooth and a whole set are teeth,
Why shouldn't the plural of booth be called beeth?

Then, one may be that and three would be those,
Yet hat in the plural wouldn't be hose.
We speak of a brother and also say bethren,
But though we say Mother, we never say Methren.

Then the masculine pronouns are he, his, and him,
But imagine the feminine she, shis, and shim.
So English, I fancy you all will agree,
Is the funniest language you ever did see.

Listen carefully to the words but read between the lines. Stick to the main points. Speak slowly and clearly. Start meetings with points of agreement to set a friendly tone. Don't be offended if the other party starts chattering away in their native tongue. (The very fact that your product was worth discussion is a positive sign.) Maintain a serious face and avoid humor. And take a page from their book - never say or do anything that will cause hurt or embarrassment (loss of face) or you can, as a sports commentator might say, "Kiss it goodbye!"

Some Asians want to practice their English skills as much as possible while others would prefer to speak to a non-Asian salesperson. This may be a form of reverse snobbery (how could an Asian know as much as a "native American?") or it may be an indication of something else. If a major decision needs to be discussed, for example, regarding the purchase of a car or house, the Asian client or customer may actually not want the salesperson to be privy to the private discussion taking place between the husband and wife or whoever is involved in making the decision!

Which brings me to a third common question that comes up frequently, "Why do Asians speak in their native languages in our (salespersons') presence?" or "Do they know how rude they are when they speak in their native language in front of us?"   For immigrants and refugees alike from any country, English may be their second, fourth, or sixth. Some of them speak several dialects of their own language in addition to English.

As a former teacher of English as a Second Language and a counselor for refugees, I can tell you that it takes time to start thinking in English. This usually occurs at the intermediate level, after about two and a half years of English instruction. Up to that point, students struggle with what I call "head translations." Information is read or heard in English, goes through a person's head where it is translated into the native language. If a response is needed, the reverse process takes place. It is formed in the native language first, then the mind has to search around for appropriate English vocabulary before it comes out in speech or writing. It behooves us to be patient as this is taking place and not press for a response.

We need also to keep in mind that Asian languages are considered "high-context" languages, in contrast to the Germanic and Romance languages which are "low-context." The origins of high context languages is in symbols, so that meanings are vague and ambiguous. In contrast, low-context language is very precise with words specifically denoting their meanings.

We who are speak English fluently take much for granted! First of all, we speak so quickly our listeners can barely understand what we are saying. Then we sprinkle our speech liberally with many idioms and expressions, and thirdly, we lack proper diction and don't take the time to enunciate our words clearly.

Last, but not least, if you have any trace of a regional accent, it further frustrates the ability of the listener to understand you. If this applies, try to make every effort to speak more slowly and clearly.

Earlier this year I experienced this same frustration when I traveled to Sydney, Australia. Whoever said that the Americans and the Brits were two peoples separated by one language should have included the Australians too! Although I had spent my childhood in New Zealand and had grown up with down under accents, I had an interesting encounter at the local farmers' market.

I discovered that I could only understand about 60% of what was being said to me and the fruit seller was speaking English! Imagine my frustration at not being able to make any sense of most of the conversation. The terms he used and his heavy accent left me baffled and I found myself acting like a dummy, asking him to repeat what he said several times! It was a truly humbling experience, but it made me appreciate what non-native English speakers go through to survive in this country.

And survive they do, by learning the international language of commerce in the world, they are able to communicate with each other and do business, both here in the United States and in Asia. Asian business people know how important it is to be proficient in English. In Asia there are an infinite number of languages and dialects so often it is English that is the common language in which business is conducted. It is said that two-thirds of the world's computer languages and three fourths of the world's scientific knowledge is in English. To access that vast amount of information, a person needs to know the language.

Just because a person speaks your language, whether it be English, Spanish, or Tagalog, it does not mean that he or she <u>thinks</u> as you do. Asians who have not been raised in the States usually learn English from non-native English speakers, from studying books, watching television, or by listening to the radio, audio or video tapes. Their native culture is the contextual window and mirror through which they view the rest of the world. Although life experiences such as basic human emotions can be shared across cultures (the worldwide appeal of "I Love Lucy" is an example), many perceptions, as the cliché goes, get lost in the translation.

Things and experiences which are familiar to us who have lived in America most or all of our lives are strange or puzzling to those who have not. Take, for example, a "knock-knock" joke. Even children who grow up in the States fail to understand the mechanics and humor of one until they have a greater vocabulary and understand homonyms. Another example is the symbol of the skull above crossbones. A survey of children conducted across the United States found that they associated it with pirates, not danger or poison. So it is no wonder that many "household names" have no meaning for Asians. A 1991 study for the U.S. Forest Service showed that only a few adults recognized Smokey Bear.

What is near and dear to the heart of Judeo-Christian beliefs may be meaningless to those of other religious faiths. As one of the Japanese exchange students who lived with our family once remarked to me, "In Japan, we love Christmas, but we don't know what it means."

Different words mean different things to different people. This is a good time to examine your current marketing pieces critically, from an intercultural perspective. If the average American is reading at sixth grade level, and the average Asian in the United States has over 14 years of education, at what level should your brochures, direct mail, flyers, advertisements, etc. be aimed? Knowing your market determines the level of your copy-writing. Are you advertising for K-mart shoppers or those who buy at Neiman-Marcus?

Remember too, that many of your limited-English-speaking clients and customers probably learned English out of a textbook. Think again before you use any industry buzz words or misleading descriptions: vaulted (or cathedral) ceilings, master-planned community, gate guarded, sunken anything, wilderness, rural, ad infinitum. Those industry buzz words are very familiar to you who use them daily, but they are a foreign lingo to the lay person.

You only need to listen to a automobile, computer, or electronics salesperson to appreciate this. Your Asian public are ordinary folks who may or may not watch the evening news on a major network, but when they do listen, read or write, it is standard English.

We might have grown up knowing what "nooks and crannies" were, but they didn't. A Japanese who heard someone say, "I think I'm going to change my mind" wanted to know how people could change literally, like a suit of clothing) their minds.

Another visitor puzzled over the billboard for the Mercury Cougar which stated "Trade your dog in for a cat". When told that "dog" was used to describe something ugly or undesirable, he expressed confusion. "I thought Americans loved their dogs," he said. If you take the time to think about some of the billboards and print advertisements you have seen or read lately and hold a cultural mirror to them, most likely you would understand why they are, like the King of Siam said, "a puzzlement."

The president of the Pacific Basin Associates International who has been involved in many joint ventures with the Japanese found to his amusement that his company was thought to be in the business of manufacturing toilets because of the word "basin."

Ask any non-native speaker of English what he wants most out of learning the language and the answer will most likely be conversation. For those who have learned our language by reading and possible listening to the radio, to engage in a real conversation with a native English speaker is a rare treat indeed.

Not knowing the language can lead to misunderstanding and confusion, and on October 31, 1992, a tragic death. In Louisiana a 16-year-old Japanese exchange student who had only been here in the United States four months made arrangements to meet a member of his host family at a Halloween party in their neighborhood.

Yoshihiro Hattori was dressed in a costume and showed up first at what he thought was the right house. Unfortunately, he had transposed the house number and showed up at the wrong location. When he knocked on the door, the student startled the female owner of the house and when she wouldn't let him in, he tried again. At that point, the woman called her husband who got his shotgun. "Freeze!" the man called out, but the Japanese student did not understand what that word meant and continued to approach the house. He was shot in the chest and was immediately killed.

While your marketing materials may never be a matter of life and death, any time is a good time to take another look at your printed materials. The average American is reading on the sixth-grade level while 36.6% of all Asian-Pacific Islander adults in the United States have a bachelor's degree or higher. In general, a rule of thumb would be: the higher the income-level, the higher the educational level, so you can target your marketing pieces accordingly.

Stay away from slang phrases that the general population would not understand. It is likely that such expressions would befuddle your Asian public even more as they have no meaning to those who do not keep up with the current lingo. What does a "summer blowout" mean anyway?

Or a "party animal," "chill out," or "radical," "buff," or "hot to trot"-terms used in youth, beach, college, or other subcultures.

A quick look at the billboards and signs on your way to work or in magazines on your coffee table will give you a good sampling of current promotions/marketing that makes some assumptions of the reader, but may lose their effectiveness in an ethnic marketing campaign.

-Is your car living in ancient grease? (ancient Greece)
 [Jiffy Lube]

-A sleek car named desire (A Streetcar named Desire)
 [Ford Probe]

-ingle ells, ingle ells (Jingle Bells) [J & B Scotch]

-Big trunk at the San Diego Zoo (automobile against background of elephants) [Ford Probe]

-We're the old masters of financial security (with Van Gogh painting) [Metropolitan Life]

-When gold must do more than glitter [Rolex]

-We have friends in high places (picture of an eagle)
 [The Nature Conservancy]

-With Crest, this is one bridge you should never have to cross [Crest toothpaste]

-A Taste. The Whole Enchilada. Follow the Leader.
 [Kemper National Insurance Companies]

-Get out of sticky situations [WD-40]

-Loosen up [Levi's]

-Polished. (picture of a Hershey's kiss) Polished off. (picture of open, empty Hershey's kiss
 wrapper) [Hershey's]

-The objects of your affection. It's as easy as FTD. [FTD]

-B.Y.O.B & B [B and B liqueur]

-Go from a Type A to a Type B personality in thirty seconds flat. [Jantzen]

In my work for my homebuilder clients, I am brutal in evaluating the verbiage in their marketing and sales brochures. While the innocent word "rural" to us may conjure up John Wayne riding off into the sunset or the wide open spaces of "The Little House on the Prairie", to your Asian clients it may suggest water buffalo and paddy fields. Consider what "open house" literally means. I also nix "gate-guarded" communities, for their potential buyers may wonder if the neighborhood is so unsafe that a guard is needed to keep out unwanted intruders. (Better to use "private", "secure", or "exclusive", but beware of using "secluded" because it may be translated to "isolated" which is not desirable to those who treasure the company of their families and friends!)

If you understand a bit more about your Asian market in general than you did before you read this book, you will recognize that some words are stronger in their ability to appeal to the Asian consumer:

security	tradition
long term	investment
future generations	convenience
in business for _____ years	award-winning
community	children
family	grandchildren
neighbors	trust
friends	years of satisfaction
prestige	exclusive
private	quiet elegance

While luxury and snob appeal will always sell, you shouldn't overlook the old standbys:

free	results
guaranteed	easy
best value	sample
save	offer
new	time limit
improved	discount
money	charter
proven	

It is only prudent to enter the U.S. Asian market slowly. By doing your homework, you can avoid making counterproductive moves. Have clear objectives, track each step, and learn from your successes and mistakes. It is crucial to measure what has worked for you in the past and what did not. For example, you may find the Japanese segment responds better to electronic media while the Chinese are more print-oriented. If your client or customer is an engineer or scientist, you can bet that (s)he will insist on getting every last detail and figure from you.

<u>Photographs</u> must be carefully chosen to accommodate the Asian sense of modesty, privacy and conservatism. The models must look like who they are supposed to be, doing what they might typically be doing. Make a major effort to avoid dress and language that reinforce the negative stereotypes of Asians. If you've done your homework, you will know which way a Japanese would wear his robe (left side over the right side, the reverse is for clothing and burying the dead), that Hindus and Buddhists do not eat beef, and that Moslems do not eat pork or other pork products such as ham and bacon.

Malays and Indians use their hands (the <u>right one only</u> as the left is considered unclean) and spoons to eat while Koreans, Chinese, and Japanese eat with chopsticks. Even the way each group drinks soup is different! The Chinese use an elongated porcelain soupspoon with a grooved handle in which to place one's index finger; the Japanese sip their <u>miso</u> from wooden bowls from the side; and the Koreans use a Western-style rounded soupspoon to drink the soup from their <u>metal</u> soup bowls.

Using children rather than adults in photographs is advised if you are just trying to get an ethnic mix in your pictures. But if you are targeting a particular Asian group, be advised to use adult models of that group. The Association of Asian Pacific American Artists can help you to identify those members who have special talents, language abilities, and skills. (By the way most Asians can correctly guess with a fair amount of accuracy, the nationality of Asians model, but nobody can be exactly right 100% of the time.)

Be particularly aware of cultural differences and respect them. If you are careless, your marketing effort may backfire on you or offend the very group you are trying to reach. For example, the lunar year is considered a time of happiness, the beginning of spring, new birth, life and growth. The Koreans, Chinese, and Vietnamese all celebrate this joyous period of the year. Any references to death or dying, funerals, loss of employment, and other unfortunate or sad occasions in your ads which appear during this time would constitute a major faux pas.

Recently a print ad appeared for an anti-smoking campaign in the Vietnamese and Chinese languages. It was a close-up photograph of a blindfolded Asian man with a cigarette dangling out of his mouth, his head positioned in front of a bullet-riddled wall. Several people remarked to me how grossly insensitive and tasteless they found it, considering to whom the message was directed. Many Chinese and Vietnamese still have vivid memories of war and executions in the homelands. I shudder to think what terrible associations such an ad would bring. Sure enough, I was later told that the Vietnamese and Cambodian communities were in an uproar over the ad and tried to have it pulled, but it was too late. A marketing disaster such as this should never had occurred and could have been averted.

What sort of results can you get with cold calling, telemarketing, and direct mail?

You can use the first two on a trial basis initially to gauge their effectiveness because not many Asians are being solicited in their native languages at the present time. By sheer coincidence, as I was working on the manuscript for this book, I received calls from a Mandarin-speaking telemarketer, calling to offer me a special discount from MCI and other long distance carriers.

However, some people may be suspicious of strangers calling them on the telephone and offering gifts, trips, and special deals. Your Asian prospects are no different. If they have unlisted telephone number, receiving such calls is especially threatening to their peace of mind and feelings of security. They may consider their privacy to be violated. Moreover, because of the reluctance to directly tell a telemarketer no, you may call three or four times before you get the message that the respondent is really not interested.

Direct mail may be more successful, I suggest that you surprise your Asian audience with a message in their language on the envelope! But I do want to point out one research statistic that I came across recently that I found fascinating. The level of education and affluence determines the likelihood of mail being thrown away unopened. People who earn $50,000 and more throw away 60% of their mail; college graduates 63%; and the more influential, 72% of the mail. On an average, Americans throw away 48% of their mail before reading it. Poll your own friends and check this out.

Now that you have created a clear, concise, culturally-correct marketing design with sparkling copy, where should it appear? If you are close to a large Asian market, you are in luck.

Weekends are shopping and dining out days and you could pay someone to place thousands of flyers under the windshield wipers of parked cars.

Native language newspapers are a popular choice among many advertisers, but if yours is the 15th ad placed by an accounting firm before April 15 or the 27th ad by a homebuilder on Sunday, yours will be lost among your competitors. You also need to be cognizant of the politics of the newspaper as each occupies a position on the political spectrum.

Everyone loves freebies and getting something for nothing. There are a thousand marketing gimmicks that come in the form of fridge magnets, pencils, notepads, etc., etc. that are useful around the house. I am not suggesting to have these go to 100,000 households in your target area, but you may consider giving little knickknacks such as these at your place of business.

Informational newsletters that help your Asian audience solve little problems before they become big problems are a good way to reach your market too. If you are a service provider such as an attorney, dentist, or mechanic, a newsletter could endear you to current and prospective clients as you teach them how to save time and money with timely tips. Make yours the name they remember when the plumbing goes out during their family party, the tires go flat, or the washing machine overflows.

Promotions, contests, and special events can be particularly successful. I know that concerts that feature popular entertainers from Taiwan and Hong Kong, for example are extremely well-attended. So are low-cost (around $25-40) two or three-hour seminars on living trusts, writing wills, etc. I once helped a marketing firm sponsor an educational fair for a developer client which resulted in several home sales, and eventually the sell-out of the entire development. Any family-oriented activity is worth consideration.

CHAPTER SEVEN

GETTING LOST IN TRANSLATIONS AND NAMES

If you want to target a specific Asian population, I suggest that you create a campaign that they will understand and can identify with-from the initial concept to the final execution. This requires careful thought and planning to ensure that every effort is made to be "culturally correct." The concept and its translation must be done at the onset so there is not room for misunderstanding.

Do not attempt to translate your existing, highly-successful marketing campaign into any Asian language. You may be taking a big risk in doing so. First of all, there is every possibility that specific words or concepts may be lost, distorted, or mistranslated. Secondly, if your campaign is based on a strictly American cultural idea, your Asian audience may be totally mystified.

An ad campaign for Pepsi Cola Company is the classic example of a cultural mistranslation. It invited people to "come alive" with their product. It was translated as "bring your ancestors back from the dead." And how do you translate Americanisms such as "big fish in a little pond" as a bank in Southern California did a few years ago? Or how about the billboard for Ford's Flairside truck with reverse type declaring "Heavy metal with jazz" or Saturn's "Goes for a song in

Nashville"? And recently I drove by another billboard for a Lexus sedan. The copy read "Revise your E.T.A." and made absolutely no sense to me, the average garden-variety consumer, Asian notwithstanding.

It is imperative to spend the time and money to have your promotional pieces reviewed by an independent translation company. If what you are marketing and selling is of a highly technical nature, you may even need <u>two</u> translators. The first would provide a "style list" of translated industry terminology. A second translator would refer to the list so words would be standardized throughout your promotional literature.

Should your product or service be commonly written about in foreign-language media, e.g., computers, health, education, there will probably exist standardized nomenclature for those fields. However, many new technologies (environment, robotics, high density television, etc.) are cropping up which do not yet have vocabularies, and these will require the technical expert to actually come up with names.

Resist the temptation to ask someone who claims to be fluent in the language of your marketing choice to do the job. An ideal translator should be someone who keeps up with the current slang, is educated, well-read, experienced as well as a native speaker of the language, and has an appreciation for the <u>culture</u>,

Your award-winning jingle in English will most likely not work either semantically or culturally in a foreign language, so you may just have to rethink and rewrite a campaign into basic terms or a different angle. This means that many adjectives and adverbs will have to be reconsidered, and phrases reworded.

Before you give your copy to the translation service, invite your Asian neighbors, friends, clients, employees, or business associates to take a look at it and read it "cold." It is important to get "gut" reactions and opinions because they represent "the man/woman on the street." Ask questions and mind their answers, comments, and suggestions. Most of us, myself included, have discovered that we can be so immersed in a project that we miss the forest for the trees. Our eyes as well as our brain skips over the same typographical error. Someone looking at copy for the first time with "fresh eyes" may pick up on an inconsistency or typo right away.

Who pays for mistakes? What is considered a mistake? Who takes responsibility for errors? Somewhere in the contract, this issue must be articulated and agreed upon. Since you cannot read the now-translated copy, try to get a translation service that stipulates at least two people will proof read it, and that you can have your associates (mentioned earlier) review and approve the work before it is finalized.

If there are names in English within your the foreign-language ad, ask the company to fax the completed ad to you before it is published. While you may not be able read the non-English copy, at the very least, the <u>English</u> will be correct.

I suggest that copy begin with a global view and transition to your specific product or service, thus providing your readers with a good frame of reference and some background on your company. After all, there are millions of American companies, and unless yours is one that has a long history

Two Asian surnames share the honor of being the shortest: "O" in Korean, and "I" (pronounced ee) in Chinese.

and well-established reputation, you will need to establish your credibility first to the Asian consumer before trying to sell to him or her.

Be advised that translating services may just do that...straight swap of words, without a thought to intercultural nuances. Thus we get curious results such as "Nothing sucks likes Electrolux," 3M tape that "Sticks Foolishly" (instead of "Sticks like crazy," and General Motors' "Corpse by Fisher," instead of "Body by Fisher."

This point was driven home when my friend Jeff Rosen asked me to review his business card that he had translated for his real estate development company. He and his partner thought that they had done the right thing by giving the translator a copy of their card which they wanted translated into Chinese.

I glanced at the faxed copy of the translation and the alarm bells went off. The first word that caught my attention was the Chinese character for "not" in the company's name, so I immediately looked at the following word. The word that followed "not" was "moving". Uh oh.

Immediately I took the card and the translation to one of my associates, an educated person who was highly literate in both English and Chinese. When I got the full translation from him, it was worse than I suspected. As my associate said, "It wasn't only bad...it was <u>awful!</u>" Although the word "properties" was correctly translated in "Plotkin/Rosen Properties", a <u>literal</u> translation denoted "properties/assets not moving", which would have been disastrous. Jeff and his venture partners and would never have known why their efforts were failing.

And by the way, be cognizant to the fact that there are two sets of Chinese characters - the traditional, used in non-Communist countries, and those used in the Peoples Republic of China. The type style you have set on your business cards is reveals with whom you are doing business, so you may even consider two sets of cards to be politically correct with each group. After your print ads are translated, have those same friends and associates read a hard copy to pick up any errors, typos, and inconsistencies.

Names

What's in a name? In Asian cultures, <u>a lot</u>. A person's name is given at birth to ensure success, a strong character or achievement, to ward off evil and calamity, bestow the attributes of a namesake, honor a parent or ancestor, identify all siblings and those in the same generation, and a myriad of other special reasons. The honor of naming a newborn child typically falls upon monks, priests, highly-esteemed or ranked persons, or simply, the family elders. Indian names may reflect social class, a trade, craft, or skill.

In creating a foreign-language name for your company or business, choose names that instill confidence. In the case of my friends, they were immediately given Chinese (Cantonese) names that sounded phonetically like their surnames, but more importantly, projected positive things. This is what Paul Plotkin and Jeffrey Rosen of Plotkin/Rosen Properties became in Chinese:

This is what Paul Plotkin and Jeffrey Rosen of Plotkin/Rosen Properties became in Chinese:

English: Paul Plot kin
Phonetic: Bak Bo Keen
Meaning: White(color) Treasure Stability

Valuable Steady

Secure

English: Jeff Ro sen
Phonetic: Jei Lok Sung
Meaning: Gratitude Happiness Life

Birth

English: Plotkin/Rosen Properties
Phonetic: Bo Keen Lok Sung Mut Yip
Meaning: Valuable/stable/happiness/life properties

The Sizzler Restaurant chain got its joyous name by sounds and symbols:

English: Siz z ler
Phonetic: See See Lok
Meaning: Time time happy = Often happy

And so did Hyundai:

English: Hyun dai
Phonetic: Yeen doy
Meaning: Now time = modern times, current

Many names are not phonetically translated at all, but rather chosen for the desirable qualities that suggest, such as harmony, security, happiness, longevity, peace, success, good fortune. This may mean that your product, service, or store name will not resemble anything close to its English name. Years ago when a new soft drink appeared in Hong Kong, the name cola became "hor lok" which literally translates to "can be happy". Luckily for Coca Cola its name easily fit in front, so was known as "Hor how hor lok" (delicious/pleasant to the mouth/able to be happy."

thousand events can be happy."

A good name can only benefit your business; a bad one may repel it. Home Savings of America's Chinese name is "Beautiful bountiful savings" and East-West Federal Savings' means " Chinese America Bank." On the other hand, Philip Morris probably killed its chances in Hong Kong because someone merely translated "Morris" phonetically without any thought to its meaning: "Mo lay see" which means "No prosperity/luck."

A new shopping mall in the San Gabriel Valley community of Southern California has a large number of Asian-style eateries reflecting the importance of well-thought-out names: 99 Ranch, 108, Champion Gourmet, Evergreen Bookstore, Great Food Cafe, Nice Time Deli, Sam Woo ("three peace/happiness"). Take time to look around the next time you are in an Asian community and make a note of the names. Create one that will project a successful, positive, prosperous image for you and your company.

In targeting and reaching your U.S. Asian public, keep in mind that shopping habits, religion, product preferences, and education are all among the intercultural considerations.

CHAPTER EIGHT

THE SIGNIFICANCE OF NUMBERS AND COLORS

Before I leave the subject of marketing, there are two more cultural aspects that need to be addressed: that of the importance of numbers and colors. Many loan, escrow, and real estate agents, as well as new home salespeople have discovered that among some Asians, especially the Chinese, numbers and numerology constitute an important wrinkle in doing business.

Before I get into some numbers that have special meanings, I'd like to share a bit of general information about the Chinese language. It has over 230,000 written characters which originated from symbols, and has no alphabet. Each word is a separate character that may become a part of another. The average person knows about 4,000 to 6,000 words or characters; the scholar approximately 8,000. There are no tenses but there are four or five tones or pitches, depending on whether you are speaking the Mandarin or Cantonese dialect.

New words to describe inventions are formed by description or sounds. For example, the word *radio* in English is five letters long, the letters that comprise it have no meaning individually. In Chinese, it takes three words to say "radio" - "receive + sound + machine". A telephone is "electronic speech" and a fax machine is a "transmit + real(ity) + machine". And the Chinese who love a play on words or double meanings are very imaginative with their puns. In the 1960s when the mini skirt came into fashion, an anonymous pundit called it a "May nay kwun", the first two words sound like "mini" skirt. But everyone realized what a wit the inventor of that word was, for "may nay" in Cantonese means to hypnotize. Thus a may nay kwun is a skirt that will hypnotize you!

Although the dialects of Chinese can be very different, the written language is the same. It is from Chinese that the Japanese and Korean languages have derived and therefore some of the beliefs regarding numbers are similar. There are many homonyms, but the variation in pitch will make the meaning of a word a completely different one. Just as in English, the word red and read (past tense) are pronounced exactly the same, but have distinct denotations.

In the different dialects of China, a word may be said a completely different way. This means that a number may suggest something good or bad in one dialect and may have no connotations in another. Last, but not least, many words have meaning only because they are close to sounding like other lucky and unlucky words. Are the Cantonese speakers more conscious of numbers or are the Mandarin speakers? The answer is like asking how many people believe that 13 is unlucky and 7 brings good luck.

In the Taoist tradition throughout Asia, odd numbers are considered to be <u>male</u> or *yang*; <u>even</u> numbers are feminine or *yin*. There are many degrees in the belief in the mystical powers of numbers and no generalizations can be made about who believes in numerology and who does not. But it is worth mentioning that between May 1973 and December 1985, the Hong Kong Transport Department was able to raise over HK$36.4 million for its charity lottery fund by auctioning off a select group of "lucky numbers" for automobile license plates.

Here is just a sampling of a few numbers (but by no means a comprehensive list) and their meanings to illustrate.

One, pronounced *yut* in Cantonese, sounds like sut which means "guaranteed" or "assured" is considered lucky when positioned in front of number eight (prosperity) or three (life).

Two, in the Cantonese dialect is pronounced *yee*, a homonym for "easy". This word is good when combined with eight so it will be "easy prosperity."

Three, is pronounced *saam*, and is close to sounding like the word for life, so it suggests life, birth, or living.

Four is the unluckiest of numbers for the Japanese, Koreans and Chinese because it sounds like the word for "death" or "to die" in all three languages. It is very unlucky to give gifts in groups of four.

Five (im) is a good number by itself as there are five elements according to the Chinese. While in Mandarin (*wu*), it is neutral, it sounds close to "not" in Cantonese so is considered inauspicious when placed in front or back of the number eight. That latter combination will mean "not to prosper" which makes you wonder how many model 528 BMWs sold in Hong Kong or Singapore.

Eight (*baat*) is commonly known as the "luckiest" number because it sounds like "faat" which is to prosper. Confucianism has eight emblems as does Buddhism. There are eight sides to the *ba-gua* (trigram) of the I Ching; eight "pillars of heaven" and so forth.

Nine (*gow*) is a popular number as it has always been associated with dragons and longevity. There is a Cantonese phrase which goes "Cheong cheong, gow gow" or "long, long, nine, nine." It is no wonder then that one of the most popular Asian supermarkets in Southern California is called the 99 Ranch Market. Nine is the square of three which is considered a potent number; there are nine rites listed in the Book of Rites. However, I want to point out that the number 9 has always been associated with suffering to the Japanese and therefore has negative connotations.

Ten (*sup*) in Cantonese sounds like sut, which is close in sound to one or the word that means "guaranteed" or "assured". Some Mandarin speakers do not like this number because it sounds like unlucky four or because this is the number of chambers or levels in hell. Care is taken that 10 doesn't appear next to the number 4 because then the combination would mean "guaranteed death." Likewise, sometimes 22 and 13 are both undesirable for the simple reason that the digits in both numbers add up to the inauspicious 4.

Knowing a few of the nuances behind numbers gives you a better understanding of why many Chinese businesses flocked to the San Gabriel Valley of Southern California. The area code in that vicinity was 818 or "prosperity guaranteed prosperity"! As any businessperson dealing in numbers e.g accountants, loan officers, real estate agents, new and resale home salespeople, or developer, you may want to take another look at the how numbers impact your business. Are some of your most unpopular models or resale homes not selling? Is there one numbered 1400 (guaranteed death, forever and forever)? Or did you figure out that you could sell my house in a minute, knowing that someone might pay an extra $100,000 just the get the number 28928 (easy prosperity, longevity, easy prosperity) in addition to having five digits, and perfectly balanced!

A glance at business telephone numbers listed in any Chinese telephone directory will reveal how seriously numbers are taken. The following is just a sampling of telephone numbers among some local business in one "yellow pages": 688-8680; 688-8612; 625-1888; 625-8686; 281-8808; 541-9488; 722-8800; 225-1888; 288-8991; 289-2833; 308-3388; 281-0088; etc. etc.

Some new and resale homebuyers petition their cities to change their house numbers. Others may believe that having a closing price comprised of "lucky numbers" bodes well for the future. And it is no accident that the new and swanky Chinese-owned Peninsula Hotel in the heart of Beverly Hills is number 9882 on its street.

Some time ago, a friend of mine who was an official at the East-West Federal Bank was the target of numerous telephone calls soliciting for the various long-distance companies. He finally told each of the salespeople that he would sign up his bank with the carrier that could get the telephone number with the most number of eights. MCI did and got the business.

Colors

Quick! What is the first thing that comes to mind when you read the following?

a. Black and orange
b. Red and green
c. Black and yellow
d. Red, white and blue

Did you answer a. Halloween? b. Christmas? c. a bumble-bee? d. an American flag? What other color symbols can you think of?

In Asian cultures, colors have hidden meanings too. Using the wrong colored ink when printing someone's name or decorating your showroom in colors associated with death may be "deadly" to your marketing or sales efforts.

The following list of colors and their descriptions can enlighten you on some of these cultural pitfalls.

Red stands for joy and happiness to the Chinese and Japanese. To the former, it also represents fire and the direction south. Some Koreans associate this color with communism and do not like the use of it. Avoid using pens with red ink in your bank or office where Asian customers have to sign their names. To some, the appearance of one's name in red ink is associated with being deceased! On the other hand, just as "red-letter" days are cause for celebration in the United States on calendars everywhere, Chinese clients and customers may choose a "red number day" to celebrate a birthday, the move into a new home, open a business, or conduct a birthday party.

Purple was always associated with heaven and the emperor in China. Do not wear purple (or white) to a Japanese wedding as this is considered bringing bad luck to the newlyweds. As purple is known to be the quickest color to fade, your wearing it would mean that the love/marriage may suffer the same fate.

Blue is a favorite of the Japanese who use it in glazed tiles for roofs on their houses. (An example of this can be seen on many residences in Japan, or even closer to us, throughout the Japanese Village Plaza in Los Angeles' Little Tokyo). To the Chinese, on the contrary, it is unlucky to wear blue flowers or ribbons in one's hair and a sign of mourning for women is to wear a blue yarn flower bobby-pinned on their tresses. The blue which printers call reflex blue, also known as ultramarine blue, is the funeral color worn by many Chinese.

Green is to the Chinese the wonderful color of health, growth, family life, wood, youth, prosperity, and harmony. Notice in your local Chinatown how popular this color is as a roofing material.

Yellow represents the earth for the Chinese and another imperial color. Taoists monks wear the color gold while Buddhist monks wear orange. Yellow chrysanthemums are a funeral flower to Japanese, Chinese, and Koreans.

White is the universal funeral color throughout the world. Just as in the West, this color stands for purity and innocence and the direction west. Indian men as well as women wear white to funerals. Koreans, Japanese, and Chinese use white and yellow chrysanthemums in funeral floral sprays and wreaths so do not send this combination for happy occasions.

Black is associated with guilt, evil, death, mourning, and the direction north. **Many Japanese and Chinese like the combination of black with red, but not black with white as this funeral combination.** Indians consider black as unlucky or a bad omen.

There are a few miscellaneous details regarding colors that I need to mention here. Women should avoid wearing red, white, blue, or black to a Chinese wedding. The first reserved for the bride, the remaining are the colors of mourning.

When presenting gifts to your Japanese friends, neighbors or business associates, use pastel colors (or red for a wedding) but not white. You can also skip the bows and ribbons. For most Asians, black is an inappropriate color for gift wrapping so resist the urge to use the "Over the hill" wraps so popular for 40 and 50-year birthday celebrations. Allusions to death and dying are considered very inauspicious or in extremely bad taste. Never give a clock to a Chinese for it has funeral connotations. Syrians consider brown their funeral color as it symbolizes falling leaves.

Giftgiving is conducted privately so as not to appear as a bribe (except at a banquet to a public official). In Arab communities, giftgiving is handled so as not to appear underhanded. Opening a gift in the presence of the giver is not considered polite and the recipient should not be urged to do so.

What constitutes an appropriate gift for your Asian clients at the closure of a home or a major purchase? For the Japanese and upper class Asian clients, signature gift items are always appreciated, although they should not be too personal. Desk sets, leather goods, handmade wood accessories, fine European crystal (Lalique) or American china and silver (Lennox, Waterford, etc.), beautiful coffee table books make good corporate gifts or for men.

For the women, I have found that elegant, <u>American-made</u> costume jewelry such as Trifari and Monet, scarves and small leather items are liked very much by wives of executives. You don't have to spend a bundle, but rather be original or creative. Sometimes finding something beautifully handcrafted, original, or unusual, (mainstream but not bizarre or weird) such as handpainted silk, can be appropriate.

A generous basket with sparkling wines or cider, fine chocolates, beautiful fruit (kiwis, apples, oranges, etc.), and imported coffees make a gift that everyone in a family can enjoy. A big, wide red bow should be tied on the handle. As cheeses are not universally liked, you may wish to leave them out of the basket.

Thoughtful and much-appreciated gift suggestions for college-bound students: books on how to choose a college or study for and take the SATs and ACTs; desk or pen sets, current hardbound dictionaries.

Another gift well received is a house plant with its container hidden in a wicker or brass pot (with its big red bow). Ficus trees, Schefflera, Chinese evergreens, and other hardy, low-maintenance house plants can be good candidates. If someone you know is opening a business, a dwarf kumquat, orange, or tangerine tree is in order, for the green leaves represent growth, the gold-colored fruit, prosperity.

Some Japanese do not like receiving a potted plant if they are hospital patients, for the roots signify a long stay. For them, cut flowers which will quickly wilt and die means that they will be recovered and home just as quickly. The opposite is true for many Chinese who view cut flowers as funeral (especially those yellow or white chrysanthemums) and would <u>prefer</u> potted plants instead.

The top alcoholic gifts are the best brandies and cognacs such as XO, Hennessey, Courvasier, Martell, and scotches such as Chivas Regal, Crown Royal, Johnny Walker Black. These can be served to guests at family, business, and social occasions.

Whether you are presenting a status or thoughtful gift, be certain that it is not manufactured or produced in <u>any</u> Asian country. On the other hand, if you are taking executive wives shopping, you may be amazed to find them interested in the apparel made in their countries that appear in our retail stores. The highest quality knits and other clothing are made for <u>export</u> and the natives never see their counterparts in their own countries.

There are other influences that may impact the conduct of business. Elders, parents, and older siblings, may be consulted. Many Chinese won't make a move without consulting the almanac called the *tung shu* that is sold around the lunar new year. Others swear by the ancient Book of Changes, the <u>I Ching</u>, astrologers, and fortune tellers. In India, astrologers are consulted for major decisions regarding business and marriage. In the next chapter, I will cover one very popular and profound part of some Asian lives-*feng shui*.

CHAPTER NINE

TRAILING THE FENG SHUI MASTER

Two men were taking a walk through an exclusive Southern California development. As they stopped in front of one particularly attractive house, the younger of the men turned to the other, "Master, here is my new house, what do you think?" His companion took a long look at the house, then turned around, looking around to scrutinize the neighboring buildings.

"Your home is acceptable," he told the first man.

"But will I prosper here?"

"You will do fine," came the reply, "but your house is across the street."

The younger man stared unbelievingly, for he had dismissed the house in question as being smaller and far less desirable than his new home.

"You will achieve a great wealth should you buy that house," insisted the master.

The next day, the young man bought the house across the street.

Throughout communities with large Asian populations, non-Asian businesses are learning about *feng shui*. One cannot be involved in real estate or building in the West without having heard about deals that were made and canceled, appointments and escrow closings that were rescheduled, or contracts that were never signed due to mysterious reasons. *Feng shui* is responsible for a good many of those reasons.

What is *feng shui*? In the introduction of her book **Feng Shui: A Layman's Guide to Chinese Geomancy**, Evelyn Lip explains:

"Geomancy is defined as the art of divining the future for good or ill fortune, from the figure suggested by dots or lines placed at random on the earth's surface. It is said that the fortunes of men depend on how well their ancestors were buried with respect to geomancy and also how correctly their own dwellings were built with respect to orientation, planning, construction, etc. according to *feng shui* or geomancy. The words *feng shui* in Chinese mean the wind and the water. It stands for the power of the natural environment - the wind and the air of the mountains and hills; the streams and the rain; and the composite influences of the natural processes."

Derek Walters' **The Feng Shui Handbook** states:

"The principles of Feng Shui are based on precepts laid down thousands of years ago in the Chinese classics, particularly the **Li Shu**, or **Book of Rites**, a sacred book that enshrines the basic tenets of Chinese religious belief. It is concerned with order, the harmony of heaven and earth, and with the ways in which humanity can best keep the balance of nature intact."

Comingled with geography and astronomy is the influence of Taoism. Everything in the world is changing, inter-related, complementary, and interdependent. Yin and yang, dark and light, hard and soft, male and female - the universe is an entity composed of two equal but different, not necessarily opposite, parts. Nothing moves or happens without affecting something else...the basic law of physics and the wisdom of Chinese ancients.

When trying to explain the most basic concept of *feng shui*, one example particularly comes to mind. A person might think about the home in which he lives now and remember the period prior during which he went apartment-hunting or house-shopping. He may have walked through five, ten or even twenty places, but how did the person ultimately decide which he wanted to be his home? In addition to the obvious reasons of locations and price, what was the final determining factor?

The answer is that he <u>felt</u> as if he belonged there, and to borrow an expression from the 1960's... the <u>vibes</u> were right. Those same "vibes" or karma are affected by the terrain, the flora and fauna, the spiritual, events, and the shape of property.

Feng shui is based on the belief that balance and harmony can be achieved on one's physical self and environment through proper manipulation. It melds an intimate knowledge of geography and astronomy with philosophy, religion, folk wisdom, and common sense. Its main component is *ch'i*, the cosmic energy that connects all living things with the land and which can be manipulated to harmonize with nature. The character *ch'i* in the Chinese language can be translated into English as "air" or "energy". It is believed that this universal energy exists in the contours and terrain of the land and in all living things.

In nature, *ch'i* is the flowing energy that flows through the land which can be altered for better or worse by man-made modifications such as roads, tunnels, and buildings. Other interior and exterior structural features that are taken into consideration of good or bad *feng shui* are pillars, chimneys, posts, roofs, flagpoles, doors, windows, beams, walls - all elements of any building. In homes and offices, it can be interpreted as air circulation. In some buildings, the air is stagnant; in others, there are drafts. Too much or too little *ch'i* is undesirable and unhealthy. By applying the principles of *feng shui*, any construction can enhance the prosperity and growth of an area; if ignored, calamities and disaster will befall.

The opposite of *ch'i* is *sha*, a negative, noxious force which is represented by straight lines, roads, or corners of buildings directed toward other buildings, in which case it is called an arrow. A structure which is sited at the base of two roads forming the letter T is subject to such negative energy, e.g. the White House! "Bandaids " to offset *sha* or improve or redirect *ch'i* are mirrors, plants, windchimes, aquariums, screens, ponds, fountains, and in extreme cases, walls.

Many examples of *feng shui* principles abound in Chinese communities throughout the country. From 1788 when the Chinese first settled in Hawaii, Chinatown streets and structures throughout the United States were constructed under the influence of this ancient practice. In the 1990's, feng shui is evidenced in the Buddhist temple located in Hacienda Heights, the Hong Kong Fragrant Garden Restaurant in Millbrae, and Ming's Restaurant in Palo Alto, to name a few. A walk down the street in any major Chinatown, U.S.A., and one might count many eight-sided mirrors to repel evil placed over the main entrances of various businesses.

Did the architect and the landscaper for the Torrance offices of the Daily Breeze know about the "killing arrow"? The building is situated at the point where two streets meet in a "T". Palos Verdes Boulevard points to the building and ends, directing *sha* right at the two-story structure.

However, at least three outstanding features deflect the negative energy thought to be rushing toward the building. First, there is a monument-like small structure constructed of Palos Verdes stone on which are anchored the numbers of the publication's street address.

Secondly, a pond with rushing water, a waterfall, and a ring of water spouts is sited directly in front of the main doors. Last but not least, are three tall flagpoles which could direct any adverse currents up and away from the building.

Traditionally, a spot which features a mountain behind, two smaller hills to the sides, with a wide view in front is considered having auspicious *feng shui*, similar to the seat of an armchair. Preferably the front view includes water in some form - a river, ocean, or lake, for water equates to wealth. In Southern California, the most sought-after property is located in Palos Verdes, Beverly Hills, the hills of Glendale-La Canada-Flintridge area, Malibu, Spyglass Hill overlooking Fashion Island in Newport Beach, and more recently, Rowland Heights, Hacienda Heights, and Walnut. All of these areas boast higher elevations with an expansive view in the front. A drive around your own city or just examining a road or topographical map can reveal the most auspicious areas.

There have been no surveys taken as to what percentage of the Asian population believe or practice geomancy, but a Chinese architect based in Monterey Park estimated that over 80% of his clients believe in *feng shui*. His office building was designed under the supervision of a geomancer and his staff jockeyed for the best office location in the new building expansion. Danny Chang, a realtor in the San Gabriel area of Southern California, thinks that 70% of the people he shows homes to embrace this doctrine. Others believe it's only superstition.

Although *feng shui* originated in China thousands of years ago, its followers can be found not only in Chinese-speaking communities worldwide, but also in Japan, Vietnam, Singapore, Malaysia, and Korea. In the United States, advertisements in Chinese-language newspapers and magazines publicizing the services of one master or another are common. But not every homebuyer of Asian descent believes in *feng shui*. Much depends on whether a person is a new immigrant, what his religious background is, how much and the kind of education he has, how traditionally was he brought up, and a myriad of other factors.

"Wind-water doctors", as they are also called, may charge by the square footage of a house or the property to be assessed, by a flat fee, or not at all. In the last case, the owner of the property may pass along gift money in the form of cash inside a lucky red envelope. By using a special compass call a *luopan*, the geomancer can determine the most favorable orientation for a person's home and/or business. Many geomancers in the United States are ordinary folks who are already in another profession - for example, teaching or Chinese medicine. Some are born with psychic abilities; others study for many years to learn their craft from "master teachers".

Basically, there are two "levels" of belief. For example, most people want the feeling of harmony and balance in one's life and trust their "gut feel" or "sixth sense" that tells them the furniture looks and feels better positioned a certain way in a room or something doesn't <u>feel</u> right. On the other hand, a person who believes fervently in *feng shui* will hire a "wind-water doctor" to make calculations based on his birth date, hour, year, and place. This person most likely will not make a personal or financial move without a consultation. While there are many general guidelines, *feng shui* can also be highly individualized and personalized.

A businessman from Taiwan who was building a 30,000 square foot home in Palos Verdes costing $15 million took no chances. Not content with just a second opinion, he consulted <u>six</u> geomancers and paid for their transportation from Hong Kong and Taiwan to inspect his property before one handful of soil moved. The six advisors came to one major consensus which became a nightmare for the man's architect: west was unlucky and all water had to drain in that direction. Moreover, no windows were permitted to face west in the new home.

Mr. Wu, an engineer who grew up in Hong Kong and has lived in the Los Angeles area for over 25 years, is not a believer, but his mother is. Wu was involved in a terrible automobile accident several years ago in which he almost died. His mother engaged a *feng shui* master to assess her son's home. The master proclaimed the Wu's residence was good for the mistress of the house but not the master. Furthermore, the geomancer calculated that the most auspicious direction for his client would be 15 degrees east.

When Wu decided on a parcel of land on which to build his new home, the geomancer was consulted again. Because a tree in the neighbor's back yard and a streetlight in front formed an invisible line that dissected the proposed footprint in two, calamity was predicted. But Wu liked the neighborhood and the community, so proceeded to spend over $6,000 in architectural fees and permits to re-situate the house on site. The master bedroom was designed so that at sunrise, the rays coming through a window would be directed exactly at Wu's bed. The right side of the house, being the <u>male</u> side, had to be larger than the left side, considered <u>female</u>. The original plans for a nine-foot ceiling in the living room were changed so that the new vaulted ceiling would increase the volume, and therefore "his" influence over "hers". Finally, a fishpond was constructed outside one wall of the house.

A second professional, Mr. Lin, was a manufacturer in Hong Kong before he recently immigrated to California. As a former classmate of Wu, Lin bought a home in the same development so he and his family could be close to their friends. After putting a deposit on his new home, Lin returned to Hong Kong to settle his affairs, one of which was to consult his favorite <u>feng shui</u> master. The master informed Lin that he would have many obstacles in the course of purchasing his home, but it was a financially advantageous move for him. In this house, Lin's personal wealth would be such that "he would be picking up gold nuggets from the ground."

For believers in *feng shui*, many considerations are taken into account when a home is designed and built, or a property is being purchased: location, history, energy, the prospective owner's horoscope, appropriate timing (of the decision, purchase, and move-in).

When the geomancer comes, be prepared to move!

-Old Chinese proverb

Using a rough floorplan sketched by Mrs. Lin as a guide, the geomancer then indicated which rooms would be assigned to which members of Lin's family to ensure the good fortune and health. Every major piece of furniture was designated to a specific location within a room - nothing was overlooked or left to chance. Lin was then instructed as to the exact date that he should move the master bed into his new home and also when the landscaping on the front yard had to be completed.

True to the geomancer's prediction, Lin did experience a great deal of trouble obtaining a loan during the spring of 1991. His wife and daughter became ill during the first several weeks after their move into their new house. More recently, Mrs. Lin has consulted the master again for advice on how to improve marital harmony in the home. She claims that she and her husband have fought daily since they moved in!

Feng shui masters are often consulted when businesses and stores are established. Such was the case when a Gardena manufacturing firm relocated from its old offices three blocks away to a building it had purchased. An advisor was engaged by a friend of the company's partners to make recommendations to ensure prosperity for the business.

The evaluation took two hours in the empty shell of the building as well as the outside property. From the accounting department to the president's office, from the factory floor to the atrium garden - every room was assessed and assigned according to *feng shui*. It was determined that because the company was the fourth tenant since the construction of the building and the three previous businesses had not done well at this particular location, unique solutions were required.

The advisor found that there were too many references to death or the number four which in Chinese is a homonym for "to die". Four benches were on the front patio, this company was the fourth to occupy the building, four steps led from the offices to the fishpond, and the two recessed spaces hiding the light fixtures resembled open gravesites. To offset the bad luck, numbers six and nine were employed throughout. Six large potted plants were placed along the window in the triangular-shaped foyer, three on each side of the main door. Six pieces of outdoor furniture were situated on the front patio and six indoor plants decorated the interior's main corridor.

In the room that was designated to become the accounting office, all desks were advised to face toward the two doors, and the president's desk was positioned so that it was perpendicular to the window and forty-five degrees from the angled door leading into the room. Advice was given on the placement of furniture in every office, from sales to engineering.

Generally the overall comments were positive or neutral as the advisor made his way through the building until he reached the end of the wide corridor to a glass door which led out to a Japanese garden with a fish pond. Immediately, he became quite agitated and in a space of one moment, the positive comments were canceled.

"The pond is a bad influence," he stated. "First of all, it requires four steps form the door to the edge of the pond. Secondly, the shape is that of a Chinese cleaver, but the cutting edge is facing the back wall of the garden instead of toward the door."

"Furthermore, the handle part of this pond should be blocked off and filled up so that the shape becomes a harmless rectangle. In addition, the water is stagnant (dead), representing a stalling of business. The garden is overgrown and neglected as is the pond. Both need to be cleaned up and a pump installed so that the water is moving. If business continues to be poor, the pond should be completely filled and an aquarium with fish should be placed next to the window facing the garden."

"Finally," he concluded, "on either December 18 at 9:45 p.m. or January 9 at 6:09 p.m., six or nine large black fish should be placed in the pond. These fish will portend the business success of the company so if they become ill or die, the handle part of the pond should be blocked off and filled as soon as possible. If business still does not improve or gets worse, the entire pond should be filled. This location has potential, but it could be manifested either in explosive growth and prosperity or total failure. It is a tricky spot so even the moving date should be carefully chosen."

While the owners of the business did not put the fish in the pond on the required time and date, nevertheless they filled the handle of the pond as well as changed the water and relandscaped the garden. From all recent accounts, the business is thriving.

In the Filipino communities, there exists a curious mix of religion and *pamahiian* (pronounced pah-mah-hee-in and means superstition). The front door of a home should face east because the rising sun brings blessings and good luck. (Incidentally, Indians also prefer this orientation for their front entrances, and those who practice Asian meditation and exercise also face east for these activities.)

During the construction phase, new homes are "anchored" by the placement of gold or silver coins under the posts of the foundation to ensure prosperity. Coins may also be tucked in under interior stairs or at the landings for good luck, and thirteen stairs leading to a second story is preferable.

Steps should be an odd number and are counted out in groups of threes: "*Oro* (gold), plata (silver), *mata* (bronze). Some substitute *mata* with the word for death and if the number of steps falls on this third word, the house is rejected. Conversely, if while counting the number of stairs, the sequence ends on the word *oro*, the house is considered to bring prosperity to its new owner.

Some of the features reflect the influence of Chinese feng shui. The "see-through" house is unappealing, as is a front door with a footpath that faces straight out to the street. In the master bedroom, the foot of the bed should not directly face the room's entrance. As in Chinese beliefs, a person who dies at home is carried out feet first.

The headboard should be at the southern wall, with one's feet directed north. In contrast, many Japanese do not want to place their heads against a north wall as this duplicates the common position for burials.

Dracaena, also known in Hawaii as the money plant, is good to have around, especially if it is given as a gift. On the other hand, plumeria is thought of as a funeral flower as it is planted in many cemeteries, and should not ordinarily be used as a house plant.

When a family moves into a new home, timing is a major concern. Because of its symbolism, moving during a full or rising moon is preferred as it portends fullness or an abundance of prosperity. A priest may be asked to come in to bless a home and guests to a housewarming party bring the traditional gifts for a new home: a jar of water, a jar of salt, and a bag of rice to ensure happiness and good fortune.

CHAPTER TEN

THE TWELVE STEPS TO CREATING AN ASIAN MARKETING CAMPAIGN

Here is a step-by-step process from start to finish on how to create a sales and marketing strategy for your company.   It's what this whole book is about-helping you to save time, money and human resources by expanding your understanding of your Asian customer or client and by avoiding the mistakes that others had to learn from hard experience.

I concede that you are the experts in sales and marketing and may already have other action items to add to achieve your goal. I am merely adding the intercultural factor for your consideration. Utilize the step-by-step list below as a framework around which you can build your campaign. Whether you are a novice or experienced marketer, the following guidelines will help you get started.

Step One: The management decides that it wants to target the Asian market and assigns the resources to implement it.

Sounds obvious, doesn't it? It's not. Like the commander in chief making the decision to go to war, the people at the top have to make the decision and the commitment to go ahead with this. Everyone else in the chain of command, being the good soldiers that they are, should buy into the plan and be similarly committed.

Step Two: Identify your expectations, goals, and objectives for the plan.

Every campaign or promotion should have an objective. As the old saying goes, if you don't know where you are, you won't know where you are going. It's like taking a trip. Every member of the company who will be involved should have an opportunity to express what their expectations are of the trip destination. They should cooperate to create the same "road map" to get to there. On the journey, the results, like highway miles or flying time, should be measurable: the sales increased by ____%; _____ thousands of units were sold; the company tracked _____ sales and _____ referrals; ____number of coupons were redeemed at which location.

Step Three: Decide on what you want to sell and select your market.

You cannot be all things to all people or you will end up like the emperor with his new clothes, reaching nobody and getting nowhere, but unfortunately, with all your mistakes on view to everyone. Be certain that the campaign matches the market, for you will be wasting your efforts and resources should you are try to sell signature clothing to five-and-ten shoppers.

Step Four: Decide on whether you are going to create a culture-specific version of an existing product/service or create new ones from scratch.

This also applies to the marketing campaign itself. Many companies are tempted to re-run a highly successful marketing campaign and just have it translated into the native language of the target segment. Resist doing this. Remember, many concepts and ideas just won't work at all in another cultural context and you'll be wasting time and money.

However, if you insist on doing this, this is the time to bring in the cultural and language experts to help you point out anything that might be offensive, misunderstood, or "over the heads" of your Asian prospects.

Step Five: Gather your management, sales, marketing, and cultural consultant together to brainstorm ideas.

It is critical to bring in your Asian cultural consultant at this point before any more resources are spent on developing the campaign. The expert must be involved from the beginning to ensure that you are not making any intercultural blunders from the inception of the original ideas.

Step Six: Have your creative team work out the storylines or concepts determined in Step Four. Choose which you wish to implement.

Invite the cultural expert to sit in on focus group meetings and to respond or make comments to the various suggestions so that the team knows what will and won't work immediately. By having the expert involved intimately with the project, you will save time and money every step of the way before an entire sales, marketing, and publicity campaign or event around a cultural mistake. This has happened before with several well-known companies. By the time the offensiveness of their ads was discovered, millions had been printed, aired, or distributed. The sad thing is that all of it could have been avoided.

I would like to offer a word of caution here. Just because you have staff members of Asian ancestry does NOT mean that they know what the expert does. Just because that person is the president of the company or a member of the marketing team does not preclude his or her making a wrong cultural decision regarding a plan. That is why the cultural consultant is worth his/her weight in gold, having access to knowledge, information, resources, etc. that your company people do not have.

Step Seven: Develop your timeline with your creative design, sales, and marketing teams.

Be sure your consultant is available to all those involved in the campaign during the creative period.

Step Eight: Train your sales staff.

This is an important step that many companies overlook. You can spend a bundle of dollars on an entire brilliant marketing campaign, get a huge response and your sales team could blow it all by turning off the prospects with greetings and sales techniques that are inappropriate for Asian customers. Don't scrimp here. Dollar for dollar, Asian cultural sales training is the most cost-effective insurance for the success of your total effort. While you're training your sales staff, include your receptionists, customer service, and quality assurance teams too. It's worth every penny.

Step Nine: Implement the campaign/promotion.

Determine whether there should be a time limit to the campaign in order to achieve your objectives.

Step Ten: Measure the progress every step of the way until the campaign is over.

Do not be afraid to be flexible and open to new ideas along the way. Consult your Asian expert for advice and suggestions should you need to make any modifications in the program.

Step Eleven: Hold a post-campaign evaluation meeting.

Don't neglect this valuable opportunity when the event or campaign is over. Bring together all the members of the management, sales, and marketing focus groups early on to evaluate the entire process. Before the meeting, instruct everyone to prepare a list of everything that went right during the entire campaign and the various statistics. Review everything that went wrong or proved ineffective. Finally, make a third list of how you would do things differently the next time, and everything <u>new</u> that anyone learned. Compile this information and share it with everyone involved.

Step Twelve: Start and build on your database of successful closures/sales.

Building on your success and experience, you now have a list of satisfied clients and customers who are your foundation for your next campaign. Create a database of these VIPs for they will form the foundation for your next marketing effort or promotion.

Step Thirteen: Follow through and start conscientiously nurturing your long-term
                      relationships with your customers.

Be considerate, thoughtful, and indispensable. Position yourself and your company as trustworthy by returning phone calls immediately, responding quickly to service calls and complaints, keeping in touch with them through newsletters and holiday greeting cards, sending them free little gifts, remembering their birthdays and the anniversary of the day they moved in, offer them discounts on services, and all those other activities that will keep you in their minds and hearts.

The return will be both measurable and immeasurable, in future referrals and sales. You will developing trust, respect, confidence, and most importantly, continued goodwill. These are the elements that build customer loyalty.

PART THREE

BUSINESS ETIQUETTE AND COMMUNICATIONS

CHAPTER ELEVEN

A CRASH COURSE IN ASIAN BUSINESS ETIQUETTE

You've done everything right. You followed the suggestions in this book and now there is an marked increase in the Asian traffic at your place of business or sales office.

Aaaargh! What do you do next? How do you meet them? Should you bow or shake hands? How should you act? Relax. This section will give you a basic course in Asian business etiquette. But, you protest, these folks are in America now, why don't they learn how to do business <u>our</u> way?

That's a fair question and it is by far the most commonly asked of all when I speak or conduct a seminar. My answer is this. International business is like a handshake - each person reaches out to the other half way. Those of Asian ancestry have made a major effort already by learning another language and moving their homes and families to the United States. (C'mon now, 'fess up. Would you spend years learning Thai or Japanese or Tagalog before going to Thailand, Japan, or the Philippines to do business there?) There is an unwritten understanding that business be conducted in the language of the host country and there is a growing trend among foreign countries that are requiring that negotiations and contracts be finalized in the native language. Those from Asia who have chosen to live and work here have already made a Herculean effort to learn English.

Watch those hand gestures. Do not bow, shake hands, or deliver a speech with one or both hands in your pocket(s). Avoid pointing with your index finger at anyone.

Learning the intricacies of a culture is a complex experience, loaded like a minefield. Culture is dynamic; there are cultures and subcultures. No human being can possibly know every facet of his or her culture, much less another's. But the more knowledgeable you are, the more open your heart and mind will be in accepting and respecting the multicultural diversity that creates the wonderful weave of American society.

There are many columns written in printed media and books available in bookstores, libraries, and other depositories nationwide on how to behave correctly in specific Asian countries. This chapter is a merely a beginner's general "crash course" or for those who have some experience in trans-Pacific travel, a refresher. Should you be lucky enough to be traveling across the Pacific, try to study country-specific books which can be found under the travel section.

Be mindful not to make any assumptions. The elderly Asian man who speaks to you with a heavy accent may be a proud U.S. citizen whose children, grandchildren, and great-grandchildren have been born and raised here. Conversely, a young man of Asian ancestry, dressed in a classic blue blazer, grey slacks, oxford shirt, and Bass Wejuns, may surprise you with a bow or a limp handshake.

Just two weeks ago I was a guest on a live radio show in front of a large audience. After demonstrating The Practical *Feng Shui* Chart, I presented the radio personality with one of the kits as a gift.

"Is this for me? Why, thank you," she cooed, "We have a tradition in <u>our country</u> of reciprocating when someone gives us a gift so I'd like to give you a copy of my cookbook." The woman made a very wrong assumption that I was not an American.

Some experts claim that communication is 10% words, 30% sound, and 60% body; others say the breakdown is verbal 7%, vocal 38%, and visual 55%. Regardless of which point of view you take, the fact is that <u>non-verbal</u> communication is an important factor in the degree of your effectiveness. Because some aspects of Asian body language are very different, sometimes contrary, to American body language, I would like to cover some general points, from head to toe, so you can at least avoid the some of the more outstanding faux pas. But you should always BE ALERT and take your cue from the other person.

We do not have a second chance to make a first impression. The first impression that anyone has of us is usually the most lasting and most difficult to change. Here are some basics on how to make that first good impression.

For starters, Asian communications is what is known as "high context"-imprecise, vague, ambiguous, poetic, symbolic, and full of rhetoric. European (such as the Scandinavian and German) languages are "low-context"-precise, explicit, and specific. What this means to us is that we must learn to get to the "heart" of a message, delivered by non-native English speakers, for often the words matter far less than the manner in which they are said.

Personal space is perceived differently from country to country, group to group. In the States, we normally stand about an arm's length away from someone in conversation and usually begin to feel uncomfortable if someone intrudes our space. Exceptions are made for situations such as in a crowded elevator or in a tunnel exiting from a football stadium.

A look at our homes and workplaces is very revealing--rooms, time, and lives are compartmentalized. Employees jockey for offices with windows in America while in other countries, they fight to get offices close to those in power or the rooms with the best *feng shui*. In Asia, the size of offices are often small and cramped; others are similar to what is known as "bullpens" in the aerospace industry. These are cavernous rooms without modular dividers where everyone, the supervisor in particular, can see and hear the activities and conversations of everyone else.

At home, many of Asian ancestry want to be close to the members of their families, and may have parents and/or grandparents living with them. There is still a prevailing thought that children should take care of their parents (and sometimes other close relatives as well) which necessitates living in each other's pockets as a matter of course. To put the elderly into retirement and convalescent homes is perceived as shirking one's familial duties.

Some members of Middle Eastern cultures like to be close in order to talk to you, or as the Arabs say, "Share your breath" which we would find unpleasant. On the other hand, the Japanese can come in close and yet remain aloof. Take your position, literally, from whom you are working with. A good rule of thumb is to follow his or her lead. If you are standing too close, you can be sure that you have violated your Asian associate's comfort zone as you watch him trying to back away from you inconspicuously. On the other hand, you may be the one moving backward if you feel someone is closing in on you!

I don't know of any Asian culture in which **modesty** is not a virtue. In some, the women are covered from head to toe, revealing only their eyes to the public. In others, immodesty is cause for censure or even punishment. Overexposure of skin, even on arms and legs, may be very offensive, and if you are a businesswoman, showing too much cleavage can send out the wrong signals. Modesty extends also to mannerisms and speech. In the latter, it is carried out to extremes and becomes insincere and phony to those of us who are accustomed to straight talking.

In American body language, **touching** someone can be interpreted as a call for attention or intimacy. For many Asians, it is considered rude. It's best to keep your hands to yourself when talking and avoid putting your arm around someone's shoulder or forearm. Slapping a person on the back in the old boys' gesture of camaraderie is generally as unwelcome as hugging or kissing upon first meeting.

To the many Asians of the Buddhist faith, the top of the head is the place where holy spirits dwell and is off-limits to the touch. Resist the temptation to pat Asian children on their heads or affectionately rumple their hair. On the subject of heads, remember that most Asian cultures revere age and the more white or grey hairs you have, you automatically earn more respect.

But do be careful, gentlemen, of <u>what</u> you place on your head. On St. Patrick's Day or any day, do not under any circumstances wear a green hat into a Chinese-speaking community or you will be a laughingstock. The expression "to wear a green hat" means that your wife is cheating on you. Imagine the hidden cultural messages sent when the Green Berets arrived in Southeast Asia!

Face and the whole concept of face, or self-dignity, is too vast a subject to be covered here. Suffice to say that next to being patient, maintaining your Asian counterpart's dignity is probably the most important aspect of doing business.

In the United States, maintaining good **eye contact** with those to whom we speak is of great importance. We like to look 'em in the eye to determine whether a person can be trusted, or if he or she is being direct. Not so in Asian cultures.

This is one behavior which is in direct conflict with Western social and business practices. Asians have traditionally been raised to bow their heads and look downward in the presence of those who are in authority. This gesture is indicative of respect, humility, subservience, and acknowledges the superior rank, authority, and status of another person.

For over a century, the bowed head position which results in lack of eye contact, has caused Asian immigrants to be misunderstood. "Shifty-eyed and untrustworthy" was a common description of a century ago in the 1800s. The conclusion of non-Asians ignorant of this cultural trait is and has been that these people were not direct and therefore undependable.

In schools across the United States where immigrant Asian children are being educated, teachers are frustrated by their charges' inability to look at them while talking. The bowed head may be grossly misinterpreted as sulking, thus adding fuel to the fire so to speak.

The Japanese consider seeing the inside of the **mouth** very rude. This is the reason that you can see men, women, and children covering their mouths when they laugh. There is a similar thought in American culture. After all we also cover our mouths when we yawn.

Another practice which the Japanese think is discourteous is that of eating while walking in public. While it is acceptable to buy an ice cream cone or little snack and consume it in the immediate vicinity of an outdoor pushcart, it is not acceptable to walk down the street eating. And a recent law in Singapore has banned chewing gum in this city-state. (Incidentally, the maintenance crew at the Statue of Liberty collects 600 pounds of the stuff each year from this one monument alone.)

Now we come to the most misinterpreted of all facial gestures - the **smile**. We tend to think that a smile is meant to convey agreement, joy, amusement, warmth, friendliness, and a dozen other positive emotions. An Asian may smile to indicate: I heard you, I am embarrassed, I do it because you expect this of me, please excuse me. To a Thai, a smile may mean he is sorry he bumped into you or from a girl, it may indicate her desire to appear more attractive (than wearing a frown or scowl). It may convey puzzlement, embarrassment, confusion, I'm thinking, or goodbye, I won't be back, as many sales people have found! The need to appear cooperative may supplant an Asian's true feelings or opinion as (s)he has been brought up not to reveal one's emotions, e.g. to show emotion would be to show weakness.

In some Southeast Asian cultures, a person may smile at you after his car has cut in front of you and you slam on your brakes, barely averting a major collision. The other driver gets out of his car as you storm up to him demanding what in the ^*(&(#%^&^! is he doing driving like that. All through your emotional tirade, he stands there with an infuriating grin on his face and you feel yourself wanting to punch his lights out - anything to wipe that smirk off his face. Resist the temptation, take a deep breath and count to thirty. Smiley is merely reacting in a culturally correct manner which is at odds with the rules of American body language.

A friend of mine once overheard the following comment which reveals another view regarding smiling: "Your President Jimmy Carter must be a very weak man, he is always smiling."

Observe the serious demeanor displayed by many Asian leaders. Televised state visits and summit meetings, notice that when American presidents are photographed in other countries, it is always our leaders who are smiling, less theirs. Perhaps it is because business is serious business and national honor is at stake, that these Asian men don't smile much. Or perhaps they have been raised in Asian cultures in which showing any emotion is considered a weakness.

The **neck** to the Japanese is considered an erotic zone and for modesty's sake, should remain covered as much as possible. Sexism and chauvinism are very much alive in Asian countries and I always advise American businesswomen to dress conservatively to avoid sending out non-businesslike messages to their Asian male counterparts. Women who wish to be taken seriously and project a serious business image should avoid wearing necklines that are too revealing.

All over the world, **hands** are used as a form of expression and communication. All over Asia, the <u>left</u> hand is considered unclean and is not used to pass anything, especially food and business cards. It is the hand that puts the toilet paper to use and is kept out of sight at the meal table.

When we wave to someone here in the States, we extend an arm out to the side, bend the elbow and bring our open palm up toward our face as if we were directing traffic. This is the way Southeast Asians call their dogs and so it is considered extremely rude. To be on the safe side, put your arm out, but with the palm facing down, moving the your fingers together as one unit toward your body.

While American women stand up straight with their shoulders pulled back, projecting confidence and control, this posture is considered very unfeminine to Asians.

What one <u>puts</u> on the **body** is also important. If you ever find yourself shopping at one of the major department stores on the Ginza in Tokyo, you may be quite surprised at the men and women's clothing departments. Although there are floors upon floors of designer clothing, the colors are quite limited--mostly black, navy, and dark grey.

To **dress** informally or act in a casual manner says to your Asian business associate, "I am not serious about doing business with you." Informality is viewed as insincerity and the impression projected is not a positive one. Signature clothing and jewelry is very much the norm for businesswear in Japan and Hong Kong for you will be very scrutinized very carefully.

Some Americans think that they are showing respect for a culture by attending a function in some sort of Asian native dress. Many <u>Americans</u> of Asian ancestry have found this to be offensive. Dressing up in this manner is as ridiculous as an Asian coming to your company holiday gathering in full native American costume.

Your **back** should never be turned toward your host or the head of household when you visit an Asian home. Chinese, Indian Buddhist, Japanese, Korean, Filipino, and Thai households are known to practice the removal of shoes before entering a home, even in the United States. A dead giveaway is the presence of footwear outside the front door or if you spot shoes and slippers in the foyer immediately by the inside of the door.

When you take off your shoes, do so <u>sideways</u>, and in a Japanese home, bend down and turn your shoes around so that the toes are facing the door. This will facilitate your departure. Your hostess may say, "No, no," meaning you don't have to defer to her cultural customs, but you can bet you earn lots of points if you insist on leaving your shoes outside the door or just inside at the foyer. (Be sure you don't wear your Sunday socks that day. You know, the "holey" ones.)

If you are a service/repair person and the homeowner tells you that you don't have to take off your shoes, be sure to make a ceremony of wiping off your workshoes each time you enter the home. Again, practicality takes precedence over custom here, but be considerate and respectful of the homeowner's customs.

Last but not least, we come to the lower part of the body. Ladies, please keep your **knees** covered for modesty. Your skirt lengths should at least cover your knees when you are standing up. Even Diana, Princess of Wales, got into trouble when she visited Saudi Arabia. She was seen sitting demurely with her skirt barely above her royal knees. By the same afternoon, she was presented with a gift of a full-length caftan, apparently one that would cover her up totally from neck to floor.

Earlier I mentioned that a person's head was considered very holy and should not be touched. Conversely, the "filthiest" part of your body is your **foot**, both of them, especially the soles which should never be directed at any person. Do not cross your legs when you are sitting down, because the tips of your toes or the bottom of your feet may be directed at someone's head, that holy area.

To do this is the grossest of insults to those whose background is Southeast Asian. Aiming the bottom of your feet at someone is equivalent to making the most obscene gesture imaginable in American culture toward that person. Be careful not to do it, your life may depend on this advice.

In the last few years, there have been news reports about men who have inadvertently directed the soles of their shoes to others. Both had their shod feet propped on tables facing other people; both lost their lives.

I tell this to you to illustrate that ignorance is not bliss and can be dangerous to your life and limb! Remember that these occurrences are no less unusual as a resulting altercation that takes place when one car cuts in front of another, obscene hand or finger gestures are exchanged, and a fight ensues.

One last word about feet: avoid using your foot to open or close a door, push or pull anything, such a chair.

On a lighter note, recently I was an introductory speaker at a Pacific Rim conference at which most of the participants were men. From the podium I could see that many of them were sitting with their legs crossed, the soles of their shoes pointing toward their neighbors. As my remarks regarding the shoes and soles were made, a discernible activity began in the room. Many of the participants were glancing from side to side, at their legs, and then uncrossing them!

Bows, Handshakes, and Exchanging Business Cards

This section will give you the basic information about bowing, handshaking and the exchange of business cards. These three practices seem to be the most perplexing of all business and social practices to those who travel or do business with Asians for the first time. With practice, you will become more accustomed to doing each of these. The more adaptable and "quick on your feet" you are, the less likely you are to be caught off guard.

Bowing

Throughout Asia, the **bow** is a gesture of humility and respect. In Japan, it is practically an art form, and to most other Asians, it is an integral part of social and business etiquette learned at a very young age. It can be executed slowly and deeply to give "great face" to the ruler of a country, or it can just be a quick nodding of the head while sidestepping.

The action of the bow comes from the waist. Keep your back and head straight, in line with each other. Men, put your hands at your sides with the palms flat against your thighs. Ladies, you have a choice and may do whichever you find more natural to you. You may place your hands in front, overlapping one another in what I call the "fig-leaf" position, or you may keep your hands on your sides as the men do.

Remember that you are not Gary Cooper at the O.K. Corral, so your legs should not be wide apart. Your feet should be an inch or two away from each other, side by side, but not smack up against one another or you will lose your balance and wobble. The speed of the bow depends upon the situation.

The slower and deeper the bow, the greater deference you are showing to the person to whom you are bowing. Be sure to look at the floor - no peeking or craning your neck, you might get a crick in it. Generally, you will be bowed to first by an Asian and you should <u>always</u> return it. The rule of thumb here is not to initiate a bow, but <u>always return one</u>. The reason is that you shouldn't make any assumptions and automatically bow to any Asian-looking customer walking through your doors. It might just be my fifth-generation American son coming in through the door.

You have a choice of responses to someone bowing to you. You may return a deep bow, a slight dipping of your head, or smile and extend your hand for a handshake when the other person straightens up. Should you choose the first, you will know how low to bow because you have determined the rank of the other person by closely examining his business card. If you didn't see his business card ahead of time, let the other person's age determine your bowing position...the older the person is, the lower you go.

How many times do you bow? The rule is to bow as many times as the other person, but be the <u>last</u> one to straighten up. Believe me, no one predetermines the number once he or she gets started! Relying on your superior instincts, you stop bowing when your partner does.

In the United States, we enjoy the game of one upsmanship. For those who bow, it's the opposite game of "one downsmanship". Each person tries to outdo the other person in <u>humility!</u> This is where the answer to the question, "How low does a person bow?" lies. You should assume the "more humble" stance by bowing just a bit lower than the other person. You know what level this is because you are bowing just a bit behind your companion. As his head is dipping, you immediately follow suit. By this time, you will have gauged how deeply he has bowed and your head is just a bit lower than his.

Exchanging Business Cards

Before you reach for your **business card**, take a few minutes to envision it in your mind. Has it been professionally typeset and printed on a handsome card stock? Are your company's name, address, and telephone number current? Is your name and title clear? Are the telephone numbers and FAX numbers adequately separated so the someone reading either in a hurry doesn't accidentally dial the wrong one?

Gentlemen, imagine yourself taking out your business card from your billfold. Contained inside are your many personal items such as credit cards, photographs, driver's license, paycheck stubs, trouser lint, etc. Those personal effects are exposed for all to see if you keep your cards in your wallet. Moreover, you <u>sit</u> on your wallet, thereby ironing your cards to conform to your rear end! I suggest that you keep them in the inside pocket of your suit or blazer which is usually hung up at the office until you need to wear it. Better still, invest in one of the many attractive <u>metal</u> (non-crushable) card holders, available at stationery stores to keep your business cards crisp and clean at all times.

When asked for your card, bring your card out from its storage place (pocket or holder). Glance down at the card and make sure of two things: 1) it is YOUR card (most of us store collected cards together with our own) and 2) that the printing is facing the recipient.

Present you card with dignity, holding the top right corner with your thumb and index finger of your right hand. Better yet, present it holding the upper two corners while giving a slight bow. If someone gives you his card with one or two hands, show how respectful you are by receiving it with TWO hands, taking it with your thumbs on the bottom corners.

While we treat our business cards casually, even flippantly, most Asian businesspeople do not, especially the Japanese who make much ceremony of the exchange of meishi. A business card represents the person whose name appears on it and therefore must be treated with the same respect as you would the person. Do not flip it over and start writing notes on the back. To do so is a serious affront. Even though you are exchanging cards over a Chinese banquet table, do so seriously.

After you take the card, look at it and study the contents. Say the person's name (try your best) and look back at the card's owner for confirmation, smiling slightly. Ask him to pronounce his name for you AND REPEAT IT AFTER HIM until you get it right. Asian names notwithstanding, European/Anglo surnames are just as challenging and everyone likes to have his/her name properly pronounced. You will be rewarded with appreciation and brownie points because you took the time. Don't laugh and make a tactless comment like, "This is Chinese (Japanese, Korean) to me!"

Once you have asked for and received someone's business card, NEVER ask for it again on any occasion. To do so gives the message that you didn't care enough about the card, the businessperson, or the business relationship. The only exception to this rule is if you request two cards at the time you are accepting one and qualify yourself by saying, "I'd like to give your name and card to a friend of mine who could use your service/business."

In American etiquette, it is considered poor taste to talk about business and exchange business cards at social functions, but that is not so with your Asian clients and customers. Networking at social and family events play an important part in building business relationships. If you are invited to any social function, by all means, GO, and bring lots of cards with you.

Shaking Hands

The practice of handshaking traces its origins to Europe during the Middle Ages. Men extended their empty right hands in greeting to show that they were not armed with weapons. In Asia, the bow has for centuries been the proper greeting, whether it be executed from the waist, or from a kneeling position with one's head touching the floor in deference to a higher authority.

Basically, there are five kinds of handshakes that you will receive from your Asian clients and customers, and being the international citizen that you are, you will be not be taken off guard, but rather adequately prepared to return any one of these types. Remember that touching, hugging, or kissing a stranger is not a customary practice among a great many Asians so you must go with the flow and do what the situation dictates.

The first is the Western handshake. Web to web, a good firm, but not bone-crushing grip facilitates shaking hands up and down. In the States receiving this handshake reveals a lot about your Asian business associate for those who have been exposed to American custom will return this heartily, e.g. an American of Asian ancestry or one who has traveled or conducted much business here. You can almost tell the professional women from the homemakers from the hand greeting they give.

The dead fish is the second of the common handshakes. Also known as the wet towel, this handshake is always a whimpy, limp, non-grasping action that usually leaves you wanting to shudder and say "Yuck!" Should you encounter the dead fish or wet towel, immediately gentle your grasp, shake, and let go.

A close relative to the dead fish handshake is the slime, also known as a low five. You extend you hand out and encounter this non-substantive touch of four fingers to your palm and is withdrawn by the giver almost as quickly as it came. Don't reach and try to go after the hand! Accept the handshake in the spirit that it was given...as a deference to American custom.

My personal favorite is the combo which is gaining much popularity on both sides of the Pacific. I like and teach this handshake because it is the most respectful melding of Western and Eastern business and social custom. The combo starts with a traditional handshake as each party extends his/her hand, concluding in a bow over the two clasped, shaking hands. Aaah...the perfect global bridge.

Last of the greetings is the <u>non-handshake</u>. This occurs when a you extend your hand in greeting and the other person doesn't take it! You are caught feeling embarrassed and foolish with your hand in mid-air. Although international etiquette dictates that a man should not extend his hand until the lady does first, few of us these days are instructed in this manner. By watching the body language of the other person or those in a group, the alert businessperson can avoid this faux pas. Should a man or woman have his/hands joined together in front in the "fig-leaf" position, you may not get a response to your extended hand, or if you do, it may just be a nod of the head in greeting instead. If the hands are at a person's sides, you <u>may</u> get a handshake.

In a group situation, be attentive to whom is doing the talking and "leading". Very often this person is what I call the "advance scout"-the translator, the go-between, administrative assistant, or merely the person with the greatest command of English. By observing how the members of a group conduct themselves, you can zero in on whom the leader is amongst them. Is there one person to whom they bow or lower their voices respectfully to? Watch the eyes of the people in the group. Do their glances converge on a central person for affirmation? You may be surprised to find, for example, in a family group, that it is the petite, non-English-speaking mother who the family is seeking to please.

We have the hardest time dealing with <u>silence</u> and always are anxious to fill it up as it seems to make us uncomfortable. Even a fish wouldn't get into trouble if he would keep his mouth shut, an old saying goes. Silence is golden when dealing with the Asian client. He uses that quiet time in a meeting to think, evaluate, judge and perhaps even to decide. (See <u>The Unspoken Way</u> in bibliography). Some sales trainers instruct their audiences to give their pitch and then shut up, for whoever says the next word is automatically the weaker one in the negotiations.

Recently I asked an authority on doing business with the Japanese what was the most important thing necessary for success with that group. "Earplugs and a mouthpiece," he told me, "especially the mouthpiece so we can bite our tongues and not talk."

Meeting and Greeting

We take many things for granted in American business. From the initial telephone call to the actual face-to-face meeting, some distinct differences in how Americans and Asians go about doing business soon become apparent. The first is that we are accustomed to our out-of-town business associates getting themselves to our office on their own. Anyone, you think, can drive him or herself to the local airport, board a plane, rent a car and drive over to the appointment or meeting. But you also know from your own experience, that Murphy's law rules!

All over Asia, business people are picked up and delivered by limousines and privately chauffeured cars, commensurate with their wealth, rank, or status. They do not experience hassles at the airport, looking around to see who has come to meet them, waiting at car rental counters, <u>schlepping</u> through airline terminals with carry-ons, driving alone in strange cars, or driving through unfamiliar streets and cities. A company will send a driver as well as one or more representatives to an airport to meet an important visitor and EVERY visitor is treated with courtesy and thoughtfulness or the company loses face and perhaps the business.

Most likely, an American business associate is staying alone in a hotel during his meetings with you. This would rarely be the case for Asian business people. They are met at the airport, dined, catered to, *karaoke*d with and then accompanied by a driver or company rep during the entire time they are in town and then given a grand send-off at the airport.

Years ago, I was charged with the responsibility of meeting, greeting, and escorting the minister of adult education for the People's Republic of China on a tour of Friedman Occupational Center in downtown Los Angeles. Years of being a diplomat's daughter had rubbed off on me and I was very aware of the proper protocol surrounding the upcoming visit.

Rounding up every Asian administrator and staff member available to accompany me that day, we made a good showing. It really didn't matter that our group included Japanese, Koreans, Filipinos, and Chinese Americans who couldn't speak a word of Mandarin, nor the fact that the Superintendent of Schools himself was not present. What was critical was the sheer <u>number</u> of people present to meet the minister's entourage and the 22 of us was impressive indeed! In Asian business cultures, the more people who meet and greet a person, the more you "give face" and defer to the visitor's importance.

Power

Power is perceived very differently on both sides of the Pacific. It would be absolutely unthinkable for the emperor of Japan or the king of Thailand to carry his own bags as Jimmy Carter did during his presidency. In a democracy where equality is prized, Bill Clinton has won his election with his down-to-the-people appeal. But in most Asian countries, there is great distance between the titled and the common folk who expect their leaders and those who possess power to behave and dress commensurate with their wealth, rank and status.

Ceremonies are conducted with much pomp and splendor, authority goes unchallenged, status is unquestioned, and the rich and famous are treated with awe and reverence. And then their subjects immigrate to the United States and must learn, speak, think, and act in dramatically different ways. Often the freedom and self-reliance, independence and assertiveness of this new homeland clash with traditional upbringing.

With Japanese or Middle Eastern clients, it is critical that the <u>rank</u> of your company representative/escort be equal to that of the visitor. To send a lower-ranking executive to meet a dignity is an insult, as you have not "given face." If you are dealing with Japanese clients for the first time, insist that all those involved in the transactions and negotiations are made aware of international etiquette beforehand. Everyone from your receptionist at the front office to the president and CEO should know how to properly behave during meetings, negotiations, and social functions.

"Why do we have to learn <u>their</u> ways when they're coming to our country?" you may ask. YOU DON'T HAVE TO, but savvy business people take the time and effort to know as much about the other culture as they can. By knowing the proper etiquette of your visitor's home culture, you are acknowledging your respect for the differences and helping to make him/her feel at home while he learns our ways. The effort you make will be appreciated as well as give you that added advantage over someone who has not bothered to take the time.

We tend to be too impatient. In Asian business, time is required just getting to know the other person first to develop mutual respect and trust. The Japanese frequent *karaoke* bars after work where customers take turns singing in front of their colleagues and business associates. Much of Chinese business is done over a *dim sum* (steamed or baked meat-filled dumplings and pastries)lunch or an evening meal consisting of nine or ten courses. In the Middle East, a business visitor is usually served tea or coffee first before the meeting begins. And it is considered very rude to start a meeting talking about business.

A friend of mine went with me to meet a prominent banker at his office to ask for the gentleman's support for an upcoming conference. During the meeting, we chatted about jet lag, favorite hotels and restaurants, both here and in Hong Kong, my banker friend's efforts to lose and keep off weight, and a entire range of other topics. This exchange continued for about forty minutes, much to the amazement of my friend.

Finally we arrived at the subject of the conference and discussed it vaguely. The banker never came right out and said that he would attend, nor mention how much money he would contribute, or which of his cronies we could contact next to ask for financial support, but I knew that the meeting had ended. Only five minutes of our total meeting time had been spent on our mission; the remaining on "socializing."

An old Chinese saying goes, "Unlike a friend, a businessman may stab you in the back." Years are spent building and maintaining relationships between families and businesses before they decide to become partners. When neglect of a relationship does occur, the resulting feelings are those of betrayal, disappointment, and sadness.

Come to think of it, we like the chance to acquaint ourselves with our clients too. Here we meet for a breakfast meeting or "do lunch." Don't make the mistake of underestimating the importance of these social-business engagements. They are always seen as providing both parties with opportunities to get to know each other better and cement relationships.

I would be remiss if this book did not include some basic guidelines regarding dining and drinking etiquette, for they are often the means by which relationships are built and cemented.

Dining Together

It is very likely that your first step toward getting to know your client or customer better will be to share a meal together. Should you end up in an Asian restaurant, your knowledge of a few of the rules of dining and drinking etiquette will help you to make a good show. Food is a major aspect of all Asian cultures and there are layers of nuances associated with its preparation, serving, and consumption.

Fortunately, the very formal rules of food and drink etiquette have been relaxed since we are in the United States, and of course you are not expected to know *everything*. However, the following pointers will help you feel more at ease as well as make a positive impression. For more detailed guidance, a trip to the travel section of your local library or bookstore will be very productive.

For example, if you are being feted at a Chinese restaurant, you ought to know that the place of honor at a table faces the main entrance. This practice has a long tradition of giving the honored guest the best view of the room and door should the meal be interrupted by an enemy attack or assassin. The host, in deference to this uneasy knowledge and his guest, therefore takes the position of vulnerability by having his back face the door.

Your host will direct you to your seat, order, serve both you food and drink, as well as move the "lazy susan". At the conclusion of the meal, you may witness a friendly struggle to grab the check or bill between those at the meal. This activity is expected and the person who did the inviting is allowed to "win" as it is his/her privilege and pleasure.

If you are the host and anticipate someone fighting for and winning the "battle" or you should be paying for a meal, it is best to make arrangements ahead of time with the restaurant to have the bill presented to you. You may also either pay in advance or disappear discreetly near the end of the meal, take care of the payment and return to the table. While any mention or display of money is considered very uncultured and in poor taste, regularly "bumming meals" off your associates will earn you the reputation of being a cheapskate. Needless to say, when you are entertaining a client, the bill is yours to pay, even though (s)he may go through the motions of trying to get it from you. In this case, you must "win".

The Koreans, Japanese, Vietnamese, and Chinese all use chopsticks as eating utensils so your proficiency in their use will be a plus. At a Korean meal you will find a long handled, shallow metal spoon with which to drink your soup, and metal ricebowl as well as chopsticks. Do not hold the filled rice bowl up to your mouth as you would at a Chinese or Japanese meal. You may use either the spoon or the chopsticks to pick up the rice to bring it to your mouth.

CLOSED for the following national holidays:

January 4	*Burma*	**August 15**	*South Korea*
January 26	*India*	**August 17**	*Indonesia*
February 4	*Sri Lanka*	**August 31**	*Malaysia*
February 23	*Brunei*	**September 16**	*Papua New Guinea*
March 23	*Pakistan*	**October 1**	*People's Republic of China*
March 26	*Bangladesh*		
April 27	*Afghanistan*	**October 10**	*Republic of China (Taiwan)*
April 29	*Japan*	**December 2**	*Laos*
June 12	*Philippines*	**December 5**	*Thailand*
August 9	*Singapore*	**December 28**	*Nepal*

Be sure to consult your ethnic and religious calendar before making an appointment with your Asian associate. In observance of holy days and festivals, many businesses close.

 BAHA'I BUDDHIST CHRISTIAN HINDU ISLAM JAIN JEWISH SIKH

Chopsticks are known as "fai gee" in Cantonese or "kwai tze" in Mandarin, literally translated as "fast sons/children", and are symbols of fertility for a Chinese newlywed couple. Ivory chopsticks imprinted with the character "double happiness" stamped in red are a typical wedding banquet favor for guests.

In Japanese, these versatile tools are called "o-hashi" which means "end" or "bridge" (from the food to one's mouth), or even perhaps to the word for beak "kuchi bashi" which they resemble when moving together to pick up food. As long as they are not the disposable kind, they are also a favorite gift to a newlywed couple.

At a Japanese meal, soup and rice are served in wooden and ceramic bowls respectively. Drink your soup by holding the bowl with your thumbs on the rim and your pinky and neighboring fingers supporting the bottom, gently tilting the bowl against your lips.

It is permissible to raise your rice bowl to your mouth and use your chopsticks to push a small quantity of rice in. The bowl may also be used to accompany food from a dish to your mouth, a mini "catch all", so to speak. Never for a moment leave your chopsticks sticking straight up in your bowl of rice. This position is used when the rice appears on a small table at the foot of the deceased at a wake. Equally abhorrent is the use of chopsticks to pass food from person to person at any time. This is only done with the bones of the dead when moving them from one location to another, and speaking of location, the Japanese place of honor is also that which is the farthest from the door. Do not seat yourself at a meal, but rather let your host indicate your seat.

At a your place at a Chinese restaurant meal, you will generally find a plate, small condiment dish, teacup, a pair of chopsticks, and a deep, oval soup spoon with a grooved handle. The groove facilitates placing your forefinger within, your thumb and middle finger below to hold the handle.

Meals are generally served one course at a time, beginning with fowl (representing heaven) and ending with a fish (representing the ocean), beef, pork, vegetables, and other seafood between. Use a serving spoon or a pair of serving chopsticks to bring food from the main platter to your own platter. If neither is available, turn your chopsticks around and use the "handles" to get the food, rather than the ends from which you have been eating.

Rice is the staple food in many Asian countries and is symbolic of fertility (as it is in America where we throw rice at brides and their grooms) and a bountiful harvest. In Japan, white rice represents purity so one should not pour soy sauce, sugar, butter, or tea over or into it. Moreover, in these four cultures, it is eaten from a bowl with chopsticks; from a plate <u>with a fork</u>.

During the meal, you may rest your chopstick tips on a decorative chopstick holder if provided, or on the side of your plate or little condiment dish. Do not use them singly (one in each hand while stabbing your food), or to point, or to pierce food. When you have completed your meal, place both chopsticks across your rice bowl or main plate. If your hosts insists on plying you with more food, shake your head, and cover your empty rice bowl with your hand as you thank him/her and say you are full.

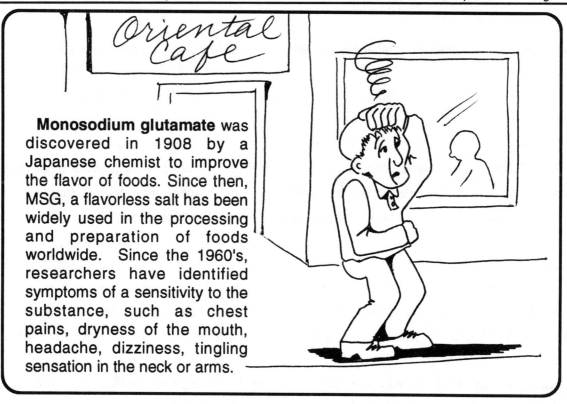

Monosodium glutamate was discovered in 1908 by a Japanese chemist to improve the flavor of foods. Since then, MSG, a flavorless salt has been widely used in the processing and preparation of foods worldwide. Since the 1960's, researchers have identified symptoms of a sensitivity to the substance, such as chest pains, dryness of the mouth, headache, dizziness, tingling sensation in the neck or arms.

A few last trivial details: Noodles may be slurped with gusto by men at a Japanese meal (but not by women) and burping after your meal, whether it be a simple bowl of <u>raimen</u> or a twelve-course banquet, is a compliment to both the host and the chef. This is true from the Middle East to the Pacific Islands. Using a toothpick is also permissible if you cover your action with your free hand.

If the teapot is empty at a Chinese restaurant, lift its cover and replace it at an angle. This is a signal to the waiter to bring more. If someone refills your teacup, with the hand closest to the cup, drum four fingers in unison several times on the table to thank him/her.

Japanese and Korean drinking etiquette is no longer as formal as it was centuries ago and today you only need to know a few basic rules to get by. The host always pours your drink and with two hands holding the bottle and you always hold your cup with both hands, while your cup is being refilled and afterwards, when you take the obligatory sip.

At a Chinese meal, toasts are often offered when the first course arrives but before it is served, as well as between courses and at the conclusion. "Kam pey" (literally "dry cup") is a popular toast for both Chinese and Japanese, or you can certainly wish for "good health and good business."

Karaoke

I would be remiss if no mention is made of one of the most popular aspects of Asian business these days...*karaoke*, the latest craze throughout Asia and Asian communities here in the United States. *Karaoke* is basically public singing accompanied by televised images and song lyrics that are generated by laser discs.

Anyone at a nightclub or in the privacy of one's home (with the proper equipment) can hold a microphone, face the television and read the lyrics on television, while singing with full instrumental background music. If you are old enough to remember the television show "Sing Along with Mitch", you are already familiar with the concept. Only there is no bouncing ball, but rather a change of color on the lyrics to guide the vocalist through a song. The *karaoke* equipment operator can also adjust the pitch, speed, and instrumentation to enhance good singing (or drown out poor performances!)

It is not polite to be the very first to perform at a social gathering, but do allow yourself to be "persuaded" by those in your party by refusing at least a couple of times to go up to the microphone. Usually the host in a private home or a disc jockey in a nightclub setting will arrange the technical support if you indicate which song you wish to sing as each laser disc contains anywhere from ten to eighteen songs.

Singing well before an audience is considered to be such an important social and business skill nowadays that there have developed a new group of businesses associated with *karaoke*. These include the sale and rental of equipment and song discs, rental rooms for practicing (<u>before</u> you have to perform in front of your friends), and voice coaching! If you can lose your inhibitions about singing in front of an audience and can sing a few old standards reasonably well, you will be regarded favorably.

Building Those All-Important Relationships

Never underestimate the importance of relationship-building. Through dining, drinking, and singing together, they are fostered. Friendships are thought to be practically permanent and are expected to continue with successive generations (yours). And while we consider the placement of a person's relative in an employment vacancy as nepotism or favoritism, traditional Asian thinking sees such a move as taking care of one's own.

Getting connected and being connected is the lubricant of the Asian business machine. We call it networking but it goes deeper than just meeting and greeting friends at your weekly Soroptomist or Rotary Club mixer. A referral establishes your worthiness and credibility to someone who is meeting you for the first time. If the person who referred you is well known and respected, your association with him or her automatically lends you credibility and trust.

A professional woman went to meet the chairman of the board of a major international financial institution. After making the appointment and showing up on time, she was asked to wait. When the businessman finally concluded his meeting, he came out of his office to where the woman was waiting. After she introduced herself and handed him her business card, the man asked, "Who sent you here?" Evidently her response was acceptable and the man's manner became noticeably more cordial.

CHAPTER TWELVE

ASIAN AND AMERICAN COMMUNICATION STYLES

In the United States where we celebrate individualism, candor, directness, assertiveness, self-reliance, and independence, many of us cannot understand the Pacific Rim side of the business coin - the closeness of family structure, the fierce adherence to a corporate culture, modesty, the constant concern for the loss of face, and the great lengths that Asians will go to in order to maintain harmony and avoid confrontation and conflict.

American communication is like an arrow, straight and to the point. Traditionally, Asians are taught not to say no directly for fear of offending the other person or hurting his/her feelings.

Although the Asian way of talking around an issue at hand initially can be very frustrating and appear to take an inordinate amount of time, much is revealed and resolved in the process. The American style of candor and bluntness is considered extremely rude for it does not take in consideration a person's feelings or his "face."

Americans can sum up the greatest difference between the two styles of doing business in one word: <u>SLOW!</u> Patience is essential, for Asian communication styles are unlike those in the

United States, and the newcomers are ever learning our ways. We insist on getting to the bottom line almost immediately in a meeting whereas our clients appear to take <u>forever.</u>

Do not show impatience, anxiety, or anger during a meeting -in short, don't lose your cool or raise your voice for you may be considered immature, unprofessional, boorish, or untrustworthy. Above all, never press for an immediate or on-the-spot decision or cause the other person to lose face. My advice is to always be punctual to your meetings, but take off your watch before you begin, and go with the flow. Triple the time you have allowed for getting the job completed or for the meeting.

While you are waiting, do something constructive. While we want exclusivity and privacy, typically a meeting in Asian circles is punctuated with interruptions of all sorts. Keeping your emotions under check and your sense of humor intact will go a long way in a business environment that values patience and long-term relationships. The most successful international citizens and global warriors are those who possess universal skills that people of any culture can respond to.

In the Asian world, self determination is not in the vocabulary. Allah's will, the gods or spirits, and other richer, more powerful people are thought to reign supreme over people's lives. We mere mortals cannot hope to ever make a difference by our actions, words, or deeds...if something is meant to be, it will be. Buddhists view suffering as a result of inappropriate behavior or desires, e.g. materialism. Consequently, fatalism is a very pervasive attitude taken by many of Asian ancestry.

A person may wonder why (s)he should work so hard when one's efforts are really a part of a grand, universal master plan over which (s)he has no control. In the big picture, it is thought that one human cannot possibly make one iota of difference. Then the move is made to this country and a person is exposed to democracy and the one-person-one-vote, government of, by, and for the people mentality. Comfortable cultural contexts are shattered and paradigms shift. Seniority gives way to merit; time becomes flexible, not a commodity; and substance takes precedence over form.

Why does it seem that so many Asians are late for their appointments? In America, we equate time to money. American history gave birth to the dominant cultural belief that we can take control of our lives and make the choices to change things in them. However, to many people whose roots are in Asian agrarian cultures and centuries-old civilizations, life is seen as a part of a larger whole over which human beings have no control. Kismet, destiny, fatalism, que sera sera - they all figure in the Asian concept of time. Things will get done in their own time which is never more important than a relationship. Time is not perceived as a marketable commodity as it is in the West.

This attitude generally changes with the increased exposure to American culture, including the aspect of punctuality for social and business engagements. A gentle reminder of a future meeting at "Eight o'clock, <u>American time</u>" with a friendly smile could be a diplomatic way of getting the point of punctuality across while at the same time, saving a person's face.

Very often, those who are at the meeting may be the advance scout in a business relationship, sent by the parent company to gather information and impressions of you and the deal. Those representatives will carry back with them not only the information and statistics but valuable impressions of the <u>people</u> from your organization who were at the meetings.

A person's <u>conduct</u> in a meeting or during negotiations may be observed more closely than his words. The Asian businessperson may spend what appears to be an excessive amount of time in socializing and beating around the bush. What (s)he is really doing is trying to get to the "heart" or true character of his counterpart or associate. Abrasiveness may be overlooked when it is weighed against the ability to work well on a team or how much a person can contribute to a project.

Keep in mind too, that the title you read on someone's business card may not truly reflect his <u>position</u> in the company. <u>In many Chinese businesses</u> which are family-owned, sons, daughters, nieces, nephews, and other relatives are responsible for overseas offices but may have to defer to the consensus at their parent (sometimes, literally) companies for approval or go-ahead on major business decisions and strategies.

By now you are aware of how different Asian body language is from that of Westerners. As mentioned earlier, a smile or nodding of a head does not necessarily mean, "Yes, I like it, I understand or agree with you" as it does to many non-Asians, but rather "I heard you."

It is well observed and documented that "Asians hate to say no." What this really means is that Asians may do anything to avoid conveying the negative directly...there are millions of ways to impart bad news, criticize a person's behavior, speech, or performance, or saving a person's face. Every one of these is done indirectly so as not to hurt the recipient's feelings or cause him/her shame or embarrassment.

If you are smiling a lot, you may be conveying weakness and your anxiousness for a deal to go through. Many Asian leaders who hold power, rank and status have a serious demeanor because business IS serious business. We in the West tend to let all our feelings show, lay down our cards so to speak, and expect our Asian counterparts to do the same. When they don't, we have labeled them "inscrutable" and "unfriendly".

Many of your Asian neighbors and acquaintances may continue to exhibit formality and reserve until they have had time to acculturate and to get to know you better. Even so, you may be addressed formally although you have known or lived next door to each other for <u>years.</u> You will know that you have earned their friendship when you are invited to a <u>family</u> celebration of any kind - a wedding, a parent's birthday, or a child's graduation.

Be prepared to be addressed as "Mr./Miss (your first name)" for a while. This mistake is common among non-native English-speaking Asians because in many of their cultures, the FAMILY name comes first, followed by the given personal name. This is true for the Chinese, Japanese, Korean, Vietnamese, Cambodians, Laotian, and Hmong. In *Asian Pacific Americans*, there is an excellent chapter entitled, "Names: Getting Them Right" which gives helpful guide-lines regarding names.

But now Asians are living in the United States and many have adopted the Western tradition of name order. To avoid making a mistake, do the sensible thing and ASK! If you are looking at a business card that reads, "Chang Li Shen," it is only prudent to inquire, "Are you Mr. Chang?" Don't complicate the issue by asking a choice, such as "Is it Mr. Chang or Mr. Shen?" Ask the question in a way that there could only be one correct answer to your question.

Many non-Asians are puzzled as to why they are consistently addressed as "Teacher" or "Mister" rather than "Mr. Jones" or "Miss Garcia". For centuries, educated persons studied hard to achieve rank through scholarship and it became traditional to address those who achieved by their titles. Calling someone by his personal name was considered disrespectful and rude. After all, the person was a highly-regarded teacher or doctor. But then, *family* relationships are so important that the very words you use to say "Aunty" in Chinese, for example, distinguishes the exact position the woman has in the family. Her title designates whether she is on the father or mother's side of the family and whether she is younger or older than the father or mother. Unrelated, close friends are also given family titles, which is only sometimes done in Western cultures.

Even on our East Coast and in the South, most young people are still taught to address those who are senior in age or authority by "Mr.", "Mrs.", or "Miss", followed by surnames, "Sir" or "Ma'am". If you see or know that a person has a doctoral degree, use it to address her or him. In contrast, unwritten business rules out here in the West dictate that we immediately use a first name upon the initial meeting. To do otherwise makes us appear unfriendly. But when doing business with your Asian clients and customers, be formal, and do not use someone's first name unless you are invited or asked to do so.

Physical Contact

In America, we touch each other a lot...a hand on someone's arm while we chat, an arm around a shoulder, or even covering a first handshake with our free hand -these are all gestures of accepting someone and wanting to be closer to him/her. When doing business with Asians in general, it is wise to keep your hands to yourself, loosely at your sides, and stay formally distanced from them when in conversation. The best rule of thumb is to be aware of what your client or customer is doing and take your cues accordingly.

Don't rush up to hug or kiss anyone at your first meeting as is the custom on the West Coast. After all, you are a complete stranger and these unwelcome actions may be considered an invasion of privacy or unsanitary. (Exceptions can be made for those of Asian ancestry with whom you are very close, who return your affectionate hugs, and who you have been hugging all along. You may think that I am nit-picking by adding this qualification, but some of my friends, upon attending one of my seminars and hearing this, actually stopped hugging me and shook hands instead!)

In the American culture, assertiveness may manifest itself in boastfulness -number of sales, who our clients are, how well our company is doing. The opposite is true in most Asian cultures. In business this is especially true. Most Asians like to play their cards close and stay mum about their achievements. For centuries, modesty has been taught as a virtue and to brag about one's accomplishments is rude. When asked how one's business is doing, the answer may be, "so-so," when you know darn well the company is raking in $40 million annually. Be prudent and discreet. Watch and listen more than talk.

The attitude of self-effacement and understatement is very evident when it comes to personal questions. "How is your son/daughter?" A parent's mumbled replay may hide the fact that the offspring has just won a National Merit Scholarship or the Westinghouse Science Award. By the way, inquiring about an offspring's health is okay, but not academic progress. Unfortunately, many newly-immigrated Asian parents have set impossibly high academic goals for their children here in the States and the result is that their youngsters are under tremendous pressure to perform or meet often unrealistic standards. Not every Asian student is Ivy League material although many first-generation immigrant parents like to think so and push their children to the limits.

When making small talk and conversation, be mindful of cultural and ethnic sensitivities. While an Asian or Pacific Islander may appreciate your asking about the health of his wife or daughter, a Middle Easterner may think you have some designs on his womenfolk if you do. Avoid making comments about physical beauty, for virtue, loyalty, obedience, humility, and good character are greatly prized in Asian cultures.

Maybe it's in our pioneer roots...sometimes we love a good fight. Not literally, of course, but we approach business negotiations as if we were the Allies going in to liberate Kuwait. The Asian side of the coin emphasizes and prizes harmony and cooperation above all. Sometimes these take precedence over truth if it will keep the peace or prevent a loss of face.

Last year I took my husband's watch for repair at a local watch dealer. I returned three times to pick up the watch which was not ready as the dealer had promised. On the third trip, the American part of me was becoming irritated and upset, and I found myself muttering loudly to the other two customers in the store. In contrast, the dealer kept his voice soft and low, typical of his Thai upbringing, as he apologized. I found my own self calming down in face of his quiet, gentle manner.

However you hold your chopsticks, the object is to get the food to your mouth! These versatile utensils can beat eggs or break cooked noodles. Don't cross them, spear your food, or hold them together so tightly that they touch (without food between).

Japanese chopsticks are usually thin, long, rounded, and lacquered; Chinese are squarish and made from bamboo, ivory or plastic.

I had no choice but to return a fourth time. On the final trip, the man went into the back of the store and returned to the counter with a cheap cardboard box which yielded a beautiful inlaid music box. He opened it up and nestled inside the gold-colored velvet was my husband's watch. The dealer told me that there was a year's guarantee on the repair, closed the box, and handed it to me with both hands. No charge, he said. I took the box with its contents and left the store. Later that week I had the occasion to price a similar music box in a mall gift shop. It retailed at $150. A month later, my husband's company needed to purchase a watch as a retirement gift. Guess where I went to buy it?

Going Around in Circles

The American communication style is straight as an arrow; the Asian way is one-way and circular. Every care is taken not to offend, hurt someone's feelings, appear contentious or argumentative, and most of all, to preserve the other person's dignity. The need to maintain harmony and cooperation sometimes may take precedence over truth. This theme is repeated over and over in *Culture Shock! Thailand* by Robert and Nanthapa Cooper as well as other books that deal with specific Asian and Southeast cultures.

Years ago, my husband and I experienced this need to appear cooperative firsthand on a trip to Japan. Before our trip, people assured us that "Everyone speaks English in Japan. You'll have no problem getting around." Not so, we found. At the Tokyo train station, we tried to follow signs and well-meaning directions from strangers to reach our destination: the train that would transport us in luxurious, high-speed comfort to Mt. Fuji.

Many natives, young and old, volunteered information and pointed in various directions. My husband resorted to writing our goal in Chinese characters on a slip of paper and showing it to several older people. All of them pointed toward a certain ramp. We boarded the train, certain we were on the right one, but to our dismay, it was a heavily congested commuter train.

Two hours later, we were at the end of the line and the last ones to get off. There was no scenic Mt. Fuji in sight. We reboarded the train and returned to Tokyo where finally a student with a reasonable command of English directed us to the correct train. It was another two hour ride, but we finally reached our destination.

Speaking of cooperation, when working with fellow employees or with subordinates of Asian ancestry, avoid directly criticizing or laying blame on them in the presence of their co-workers. Doing so will cause a major loss of face and the recipient of the dressing down will be mortified, deeply shamed and humiliated. Address the issue or problem publicly but obliquely. If there is fault to be found, find it privately by calling each person into the office individually. If you have many Asians working with or for you, not pointing the finger at any one person or putting the responsibility on anybody provides the entire group with the opportunity to solve the problem and save "face" at the same time.

Out here in the West, we have a reputation of being very open and friendly at the onset of a relationship, but if a customer or client calls six months to ten months later, we may have completely forgotten him or her. This is a grave mistake that reinforces many Asians' shared opinion of Americans. "They only come to seek us out if they have something to sell," is a comment often heard.

Which brings us to maintaining the relationship after the sale. Trust and respect have always been earned the traditional way - one has to work for them. When doing business with the Asian market, this is even more true. Your company can spend millions on a marketing campaign, but nothing is as effective as one satisfied client or customer picking up Alexander Graham Bell's invention and broadcasting your name or your company's name to every single family member and friend. These cannot be measured in terms of dollars because most Asian business stems from <u>referrals</u>. At the 1989 Building Industry Show, the representative from Shea Homes announced that the company had tracked their sales and found that every successful conclusion brought <u>five</u> referrals. One of my clients countered that her Asian clients brought in an average of <u>eleven</u> referrals each.

Going that extra distance in terms of service and follow-up will keep you head and shoulders above your competition. It is projected that 2 million more Asians will immigrate to the United States by the year 2000. Chances are great that your clients have friends and family members who are planning to or are in the process of moving here. If the old 80/20 rule holds true, that 80% of your business comes from 20% of your customers, then it is doubly true with the Asian network.

You can save time and money by maintaining a thoughtful relationship with past clients and customers. Ask if they know of anyone who would like to live near them or want to get as good a deal as they did on their purchase from you, and may you have that name. I do not advise, however, using a cash incentive for referrals because this strategy goes against the grain of the close family/friendship ties and will probably be perceived as "selling out" or being disloyal. Rather, split the incentive and reward both your source and the referral to create a win/win situation.

Of course your product has to be one of quality to start with in the first place. With all due respect to our local aerospace companies, I contend that the Asian grapevine is the fastest communications system on earth! One phone call to a friend or family member can make or break you or your company's reputation in a community. Keep your word in all of your dealings; go for extra credit when doing your homework; and always focus on building a long term relationship.

Your Community Involvement

You may not realize it, but as a member of your community, you may be expected to be an instant expert about it. As you engage in small talk with your Asian customer, listen carefully to discern his needs and concerns. If you can, be prepared to share information about your community, especially the local educational system, the reading and CAP scores, the number of graduates who went on to college and university study from the local high schools - these are the details that are close to the hearts of Asians. Of secondary importance are the whereabouts of the local libraries, music stores (traditional kind that sell instruments and sheet music, and is a source for lessons), ethnic markets and restaurants, temples and churches, tennis and golf facilities, hospitals and civic offices. By offering your help or resources, you will gain the trust, respect, and esteem so vital to relationship-building.

Keep that database current on all of your clients or customers and remember them with a call, card, or small holiday gift at least once a year. Take an interest and keep in touch with your Asian clientele. On major holidays, earn brownie points by remembering them. You can keep track of ethnic celebrations by sending for the free *Ethnic Calendar*, published annually by the City of Los Angeles Human Relations Commission, Room 1000, City Hall, Los Angeles, California 90012. Telephone (213) 485-4495. The California Office of Tourism (1211 L Street, Suite 103, Sacramento, CA 95814 (916) 322-1396) publishes a free *Calendar of Ethnic Events* for the state each year. In addition, the National Conference of Christians and Jews (71 Fifth Avenue, New York, NY 10003) also publishes *A Calendar of Religious Holidays and Ethnic Festivals*.

Be knowledgeable about your local demographics and which groups reside or work in the community in which your business is located. Stay aware of various ethnic holidays monthly and get involved in planning and implementing events to help celebrate them. Get involved. Your visibility and willingness to learn will endear you to the other volunteers. Try to give coupons and discounts, or not charge money for your assistance or services - this is the American way. Asians expect free help from their friends, or at least a healthy courtesy discount.

If you and your business plan to be in the community and the Asian market as a long-term player, you cannot only make money in their communities. You must keep earning their respect and trust <u>by giving something back</u> to those who patronize your business. There are many deserving community-based organizations serving the Asian populations. Research them and make your financial contribution to several of them, or donate goods or services. The word will spread quickly about your support and good will.

Getting involved will enable you to learn more about various cultures and seeing your co-workers as individuals. Those who work alongside you will remember that you helped them and will tell others about your efforts. The Lunar Year (celebrated by the Chinese, Koreans, and Vietnamese), Buddha and Confucius' birthdays and a multitude of national days are listed on the Ethnic Calendar. Most Asians will appreciate your participating in local events.

It is only when community businesses make money off the residents in an area without giving something back that resentment can build up. Hire local young people, sponsor a local sports team, a health, educational, or book fair, free crime prevention programs or a parking lot carnival - the possibilities are numerous. The reporters for foreign-language newspapers cover community events and can be excellent resources. There are many organizations in ethnic communities deserving of your time, financial or human resources: professional, senior citizens, cultural, youth, political activist, etc.

In return for your sponsorship of an event, you can ask for frequent mention in pre-event literature and in subsequent news releases to the media; a chance to make some promotional or inspirational remarks on the stage at the microphone during the event; or your company's name highly visible on banners, balloons, and imprinted gift items.

Lynn Choy Uyeda of Lynn Choy Uyeda and Associates gives these tips for sponsoring a special event:

1.   Build a good working relationship with the event organizer who is in charge and who will in turn delegate the work to his staff. A letter, a follow-up call, and a get-acquainted meeting are essential.

2.   Be certain that all parties understand what you expect in return for the sponsorship.

3.   Pay attention to details and leave nothing to chance.

4.   Initiate contacts with community organizations that are worthy of your support.

Lunar New Year

You don't have to spend a lot of money to show respect for your local ethnic population. For example, the lunar new year usually falls between January 21 and February 20 on the Gregorian calendar. Businesses close down and everyone celebrates by taking several days off. There are family obligations to attend to, meals to cook, homes to clean, debts to pay off, haircuts to get, and new clothes to purchase - all in anticipation of New Year's Day.

The operative color is red for good luck and gold for prosperity, and luckily, this major holiday occurs right before Valentine's Day. A trip to any Chinatown will reap many inexpensive decorations that you could put up in your place of business. You may have a giveaway of Chinese wall calendars (buy them at least six weeks before because they sell out quickly.) or just display a basket at the counter, lined with a red cloth napkin and filled with tangerines (preferably with stem and leaves). Invite your customers to take two of the fruits and wish them a happy new year.

Give the children who come with their parents to your place of business two shiny new dimes or quarters in red envelopes. Again, these can be purchased for about two dollars for two dozen in grocery, book, and gift stores in areas that have large Chinese or Vietnamese populations. Or you can send a new year's card to your Asian clients, customers, friends, and neighbors. This is a very popular practice and there are a wide variety available. The celebration may continue for two weeks.

Most Indians celebrate the new year on January 1, and a second holiday feted regionally by the many different religious in the form of family gatherings and feasts. The Japanese observe Shogatsu ("first day" and "first month") through January 3 by cleaning their homes for the Toshigami, the spirit associated with the incoming year. Sending new year cards to one's family and friends is a popular custom, very much like our tradition of Christmas cards.

Around the time of the Jewish Passover and the Christian Easter, Laotians celebrate their new year. About two weeks before, celebrants throw water at each other to "wash away the bad" of the old year. Two days before and on New Year's day, Buddhists visit their temples for cleansing of their minds and bodies, and to receive blessings from monks garbed in saffron-colored robes. Traditional foods at this time are curries, meats, stewed or pickled vegetables, spicey sauces, sweet, sticky rice, and soy milk.

Year of the Rooster (4691)	January 23, 1993
Year of the Dog (4692)	February 10, 1994
Year of the Boar (4693)	January 31, 1995
Year of the Rat (4694)	February 19, 1996
Year of the Ox (4695)	February 7, 1997
Year of the Tiger (4696)	January 28, 1998
Year of the Hare (4697)	February 16, 1999
Year of the Dragon (4698)	February 5, 2000
Year of the Serpent (4699)	January 27, 2001
Year of the Horse (4700)	February 12, 2002
Year of the Ram (4701)	January 30, 2003

Another major celebration in Japanese, Korean, Vietnamese and Chinese communities is the Harvest Moon Festival which occurs on the 15th day of the 8th month on the lunar calendar. It is the one night of the year during which the moon is believed to be at its fullest and brightest.

During "*Chusok*" (harvest festival) Korean families wire money home, give money orders and gift certificates, exchange presents of housewares with friends and relatives, and purchase new clothing for children and grandchildren. Foods that symbolize a good harvest, such as rice cakes, wheat, chestnuts and persimmons, are traditional at this time of year.

Chinese families reunite for a family meal together, followed by a moon-viewing (thought to bring good luck) in the garden while drinking tea, partaking of fall fruits, and sharing stories of Chang O who stole the pill of immortality and was banished from earth to the moon. A popular delicacy of this festival is the moon cake: a thin baked shell filled with red bean paste, lotus seed paste, or mixed fruits and nuts.

These are but two of the major celebrations; there are many more that you can celebrate with your community or neighborhood if you have been checking your ethnic calendar. Talk to your present customers and clients and listen to them. Ask questions. Be aware of changes in decorations or the items for sale at the ethnic businesses you patronize, e.g. restaurants, markets, retailers. Read **Asian Week, Asian Wall Street Journal, Rafu Shimpo**, and the newspapers of major cities in the United for clues to upcoming festivals. (The <u>food</u>, <u>metro,</u> <u>lifestyle</u> sections are often good resources).

Wishing You A Very Prosperous Year of the Rooster!

恭喜發財

새해 복많이 받으 십시요

CHÚC MỪNG NĂM MỚI

HAPPY NEW YEAR!!!

CHAPTER THIRTEEN

SUCCESSFUL SELLING

At a recent seminar I conducted for over thirty retailers at a local mall, a jeweler told the story of his experience with an Asian customer. A young man and his fiancee came into the store to look at engagement rings. Once they had made their decision, they returned many times over the period of a month to look at the ring, each time bringing various relatives with them, including the man's mother. The ring was ooohed and aahed over, but not bought.

The jeweler had scheduled his vacation months in advance and was eager to close the sale before his departure. The day before he left, the couple came into the store again, looked and tried on the ring for the umpteenth time, had it returned to the display case and were getting up to leave the store.

The jeweler went up to them and blurted out, "Look, I'm going on vacation for three weeks starting tomorrow. If you want to buy the ring, come in anytime. You don't have to bring your mother with you."

The man and his fiancee left the store and never returned. The ring retailed at $5,000.

An Asian woman was interested in a new car and went to a dealer on the way to a friend's home. Although she had test-driven the identical model at a car dealership near her own home, she wanted to do so again before making a final decision. At the showroom, she was greeted by a salesman who politely nodded to her in greeting and followed her around, continuously talking about the car's features. Then they went for a test drive.

The salesman drove the automobile out of the parking lot and then pulled over to the curb so that he and his prospective customer could change places. Once the woman was behind the wheel, the following conversation took place.

"Before you start, look me in the eye and tell me that you're not just taking me for a ride today. My wife would love it if I made this sale, but you are way out of your area. Why didn't you go to the dealership XYZ Auto Plaza near your home?"

Although the woman felt offended by the man's words, she answered that she was on her way to her friend's home for dinner, had miscalculated the driving time, and had an extra half hour or so before her engagement.

"All right, I suppose. I used to be a driver's education teacher," said the salesman, "All you have to do is point the car to where you want it to go," he said as they took off.

The salesman kept up a constant stream of chatter, directions, and instructions as they drove onto the highway and surface street for twenty-five minutes before returning to the lot.

"I can give a great deal on this car," the man told the woman as she was getting into her own car. No way, she thought as she drove away. The price <u>was</u> better than at her local dealership, but she never called the salesman back. His offensive remarks had just destroyed his chance to make a sale on a $45,000 Lexus.

A family group exited the mini van in the exclusive, gated residential neighborhood: a couple and their two children. As the parents were occupied with viewing the various models, the children played outside, climbing on and jumping off the low retaining wall surrounding the flowerbeds. Seeing this, a security guard yelled loudly to the children to get off the wall.

Suddenly the two parents came storming out of one of the houses, trailing the salesperson.

"You should have told <u>me!</u>" said the father to the guard angrily as he and his wife bustled his children off to his car.

The salesperson watched as her $1.5 million sale and comfortable commission drove off.

An Asian man shopping for a new car went into an automobile dealership. After answering a few questions, the salesperson asked Mike if he would like to leave his own car at the showroom and drive the new car home.

American body language is open.

"Would you like to keep my car keys?" the prospect asked.

The salesperson replied no and Mike drove the demo car off the lot home. The next day he came back to pay for the car as well as pick up his old one. Twenty years later, Mike still repeats the story with wonderment of how the salesperson <u>trusted</u> him with the car.

> *Experience is a hard teacher.*
> *It gives the test before the course.*

Good marketing and word of mouth may get your target prospects through your door, but intercultural insensitivity may lose you the sale. The four incidents related are true, and resulted in lost sales and destroyed public relations. No company can afford to lose business due to ignorance, but not to learn from one's mistakes is foolish.

I read the following statistics somewhere:

96% of unhappy customers never complain.

91% of dissatisfied customers take their business elsewhere.

82% of customers are lost due to poor performance or bad attitude

By now, you will have realized that these statistics may be even higher when applied to the Asian American who may have been brought up traditionally. A complaint or negative comment lodged against a business will cause a loss of face to that business. However, with acculturation, the reluctance to speak up or to complain diminishes, and some Asians become very vocal.

Throughout this book, I have covered many of the intercultural aspects of doing business with Asian clients, customers, and even associates and colleagues, but there's more. Each year millions of dollars are spent on training and many account executives attend several seminars annually. Those who have had the opportunity to participate in an <u>intercultural</u> training have been responsive and appreciative of this new knowledge. These folks know that their companies have invested time and money to help them do their jobs more efficiently, effectively, and productively. The bottom line is that everybody has benefited: management, staff, the customer, the business.

Here are some other suggestions to incorporate into your repertoire of selling techniques. Be aware that some of them may be contrary to those you have learned or used in the past with non-Asian prospects. Think about how each fits your personal style and implement those that you feel comfortable with.

1. If you are seated at your desk, get up and walk around it to greet your customer.
2. If you are on the telephone, be sure to acknowledge the presence of the person, ask him/her to wait, and end your call promptly.
3. Be friendly and very knowledgeable about your product.
4. Address your prospect by surname, preceded by "Mr.", "Ms.", or "Dr." Do not use first names.
5. Speak clearly, articulating your speech. Avoid using unfamiliar terminology and industry lingo.
6. Bow only when bowed to. Shake hands with anyone who extends one.

7. Be conservative and professional in your speech, manner, and dress.

8. Be an empathetic listener. Try your best to understand the message behind the halting speech.

9. Keep in mind that your goal is not just a quick sale, but a long term relationship that may lead to future referrals.

10. Don't try to sell every minute. If the prospect is silent, show respect and be quiet too.

11. If you are female and a male customer is looking at samples such as in a carpet showroom, sit down on the floor at his level, not above him.

12. Male sales associates should make a point of introducing their female associates to give them status and credibility.

13. If you are going to be out of the office for <u>any</u> reason, be sure your associate(s) knows the customers you have been working with and can cover for you. Don't let any of your potential sales "fall through the cracks."

14. Be careful when using humor...it is not universal and any sort of teasing may be misinterpreted or misunderstood, however innocent or affectionate.

15. Look around your sales office or store through the eyes of the customer. Are there seats for older members of a family or something for the children to do while they are waiting?

16. Offer a cup of tea or coffee graciously. Acknowledge and apologize to any waiting customer if you cannot give your attention right away.

17. If a child is misbehaving, destructive, or out of control at your place of business, <u>quietly</u> and <u>discreetly</u> approach the mother or father and point out the <u>safety</u> hazards, etc. Do not point out the undesirable behavior in a loud, public voice, but rather project your concern for the child's welfare.

18. Wait patiently if the customer and his family resort to speaking in their native language, or become loud and emotional in their discussions. Things are not what they appear and the very fact that they are discussing the purchase can be a very positive sign.

19. Do not make any negative comments or criticize competing businesses.

20. Ask for the correct pronunciation of the customer's name before (s)he leaves ("Could you say your name again please?"), reintroduce yourself and say his/her name ("Thanks, Mr./Ms. Kim, I'm Tony Johnson."), and invite him/her back ("If you have any questions or want to bring your family, you're welcome any time."

21. Walk your customer/client to the door or elevator and say your farewells there. Hold

the door open for your guests.

22. Give a nod, slight bow, or handshake as a parting gesture and invite them back with warmth and welcome.

CHAPTER FOURTEEN

CATCHING THE SILVER WAVE OF THE 1990S

What's ahead for the U.S. Asian market? If the demographers are correct, I envision an aging population that is more Americanized, for the foreign-born immigrants from across the Pacific will decline 62 percent in the next decade, and 49 percent thirty years hence. In the coming years, the number of elderly Asian women over the age of eighty will increase 325% by the year 2010. Generally, however, the next decade will see more Asian men in the 45 to 64 year-old bracket, and more Asian women in the 50 to 64 year-old range.

As with the general population, this emerging market is a huge one, begging to be addressed. Once again, those businesses that show ingenuity, innovation, and flexibility will be able to move quickly to fill the niche.

By the mid 1990s, many Americans and residents of Asian ancestry will have reached middle age, have held a number of jobs and/or owned several businesses, properties, homes, and cars. Their children will most likely be at least of high school age or older; a growing number will becoming grandparents.

In the Asian tradition, these folks will want to continue living in their own homes in which they have emotionally as well as financially invested. They may resist moving from the comfortably familiar neighborhoods and communities in which they raised their children. Other empty-nesters will prefer to shed the care and maintenance of their four or five-bedroom houses, and may sell, give, or co-own it with their adult children, and then move into smaller quarters.

There will be a great need for "culturally sensitive" retirement communities for the Asian elderly, as there is today. Among my own friends and family, for example, there are many over the age of 65, most of whom are currently healthy and living independently. These "junior seniors" (up to age 80), are active and still able to drive themselves around to shop, meet friends for meals, attend worship services, and travel.

Those students of the 1920s, 30s, and 40s who left their motherlands to study, work, live, and raise their families in the United States are now already enjoying their retirement years. Those who have experienced the decline in their health or have lost a spouse may now move in with their "sandwich generation" who are primarily female children between the ages of 40 and 60. These women are likely to be professionals in their own fields of interests and who are caregivers to both their own children as well as their aging parents.   The numbers of multi-generational households will increase in time.

> The home with a grandparent harbors a jewel.
> -Chinese proverb

While elderly Americans are sometimes neglected or ignored by their families, the Confucian tradition of honoring and caring for one's parents will prevail. While not as fiercely independent and individualistic as non-Asian Americans, naturalized citizens will expect and look forward to being looked after *in their declining years* by their families, but not necessarily in the home. However, until they are infirm, this group will be Americanized enough to live comfortably "in place" first, and not expect or demand(as in preceding generations) that their families take them in. This acculturalization also enables them to live in <u>any</u> community, whether it has a large Asian population or not.

For example, I have made some observations about the friends of my parents and in-laws who are now living in the United States. They cherish their class reunions and gatherings of fellow alumni from Chinese Christian colleges and universities. They worry about each other and keep in touch by letter and telephone regularly to share the current news about their families and friends. Both men and women experience tremendous grief and loss for their friends who are now beginning to lose their spouses to illness and death.

Many, while they consider themselves healthy and able, are traveling more than ever, a luxury they could not afford during their working or children-raising years. There is a tremendous interest in retirement communities that can provide services to those at the various stages: independent living, assisted living, catered living, supervised leisure living, and skilled nursing care.

These junior seniors are taking a proactive course in planning their later years, and the comment I hear over and over is, "We don't want to be a burden to our children." They are educated, practical, and thoughtful decision-makers who realize the importance of keeping themselves occupied, productive, and healthy.

Many longtime friends and schoolmates have immigrated to the same geographical areas and enjoy each other's company and their shared past. They want to live in proximity to each other, close to convenient services and shopping, but most importantly, to their children and grandchildren. The "senior seniors" (over age 80) who can no longer drive or get around on their own, will rely on their offspring, grandchildren, nieces, nephews, and others to transport them to various functions and gatherings, which are characterized by reminiscing and commiserating. A lot of their activities may be clustered around weekends, the only spare time available for their working children to transport them here and there.

The aging Asian consumer will probably not be swayed by prestige or ego-centered marketing. They have reached a stage in life when material things now matter far less to them than their families, old friends, and good health. Their lives and homes are simpler, but may still be cluttered with family photographs, mementos, and other items of sentimental value. Because many of them were children of the Depression era as well as of traditional Confucian upbringing, they are frugal when spending on food and clothing.

But when it comes to their children and grandchildren, they are very likely to be indulgent and generous. Domestic and international travel will be very popular, and they will most likely travel by air, rail, or bus with old friends. It is not unusual to find many Asian seniors who habitually spend different parts of the year with various offspring in different parts of the country, depending on the climate.

Ethnic health care will become a booming business in the next decade. Here are a few intercultural pointers for those in the business:

- Recognize that many female Asian patients are shy about their bodies, and if possible, assign a female caregiver to patients to minimize embarrassment.

- Some patients may rather "suffer in silence" than ask for pain relief or complain about discomfort

- Involve family members as much as possible in matters of diet, the giving of medications, recovery, and rehabilitation.

- Respect native customs and beliefs, and acknowledge that many patients use a combination of both Western and traditional treatment to get well.

Because so many Asians will have lived in the United States for many years, they will have become comfortably acculturated. For example, as new immigrants they may have preferred to eat out at ethnic restaurants, they now may enjoy dining out with their children and grandchildren at non-Asian establishments. And the seniors have the disposable income with which to pay for meals.

They will continue to subscribe to native-language newspapers but watch the evening news in English. The retired professionals will be a good market for home electronics such as personal computers, home entertainment, and home and automobile security devices.

To maintain good mental and emotional health, Asian seniors will pursue leisure time activities such as gardening, needlework, reading, cooking, correspondence, photography, music, watching videos and television, and visiting with their friends and families. Many such hobbies will be those enjoyed in their youth. Most likely, their choice of exercise will be low impact and aerobic, such as walking, ta'i ch'i and chi-gong and other traditional forms, over the more strenuous sports, such as tennis and skiing, which they enjoyed in their younger days. They are aware of their own mortality and want to live long lives surrounded by their families.

Because of their accumulation of education, employment, business and life experiences, Asian senior citizens will be savvy consumers, responsive to price, value, information, and emotional stimuli. They may be brand loyal, but they will be open to new products and services. More than ever, they will want to give their business to "that nice man" at a certain store and pay a little more. They will remember thoughtfulness, courtesies, rudeness, and slights.

Time will have taken on a different form for them as they will take longer to make their decisions which will be far less impulsive than in their youth. Marketing strategies that stress urgency will diminish in effectiveness for this group. Words such as "enjoyment" and "easy to understand and use" will become more effective that "limited-time offer" or "place your order today."

Once again, word-of-mouth marketing will prevail, becoming as important as the trust cemented over decades of friendships. The circle of business relationships developed over the years will expand to include professionals with whom they have connections, now younger relatives and the children of their friends. All those years you spent nurturing that long-term relationship will continue to pay dividends. After all, how could they forget longtime neighbors and business associates such as the person who sold them their first house or car, watched their children develop to adulthood, and who has kept in touch with them all these years?

If you are in retail, consider the physical changes of the aging population and modify your business accordingly. Forget the mood lighting, blaring speakers, and crowded spaces. You will need better lighting for failing eyes, wider aisles for the slower shoppers, or those with walkers or are wheelchair bound; chairs for customers to rest in; softer music through the sound systems. Your sales personnel should be trained to be empathetic, patient, and caring. They should lower the pitch of their voices when they speak and decrease the speed of their speech.

Research has shown that in aging, vision is the first to deteriorate, then hearing, followed by motor and cognitive skills. Businesses that provide vision correction, cataract surgery, and related services will be great demand, as will those dealing in hearing aids and audio enhancements. Pacemakers and footwear, warm inner clothing and safety tub and shower bars, home shopping, mail, and shopping services-the possibilities are infinite.

Other areas with great potential are any which deal with improving the quality of life for the burgeoning numbers of Asian and non-Asian senior citizens. Because of their interest their health, environment, security, and their ever-important families, the fields of health and nursing care, legal, tax, and investment services, and leisure activities will grow.

The need will be great for homes designed to accommodate the Asian senior citizen population. While they will not require proximity to schools, they will want safety and community services. Many may wish to live near cultural or educational facilities. They will want large second and third bedrooms with generous storage for their individual hobbies and overnight stays by younger family members.

Flooring and task-specific lighting will be important to those with diminished eyesight. Smoke detectors, non-slip flooring, wider doors, fewer stairs and inclines, spacious and safe bathrooms should all be standard. Attached, shared housing and "granny flats" are other options that show much promise for the future.

The three-car garage may give way to the single car storage, or no-car residences. Product designers can anticipate the wave and begin changing details on telephones, remote controls for home entertainment equipment, light switches, bathroom fixtures, and a whole array of other everyday devices.

Think about your business and how it can tap into today's Asian market and that of the future.

AFTERWORD

THE AMBASSADOR IN US ALL

In the final analysis, how <u>do</u> people learn about other cultures? In today's high-tech age, we get our information instantly through the magic of space-age electronics-computers and communications satellites which can transmit sounds and sights at tremendous speeds. Or we can learn about each other with the old, tried and true, low-tech means: reading, traveling, attending classes, through conversation, listening and observation.

When you think about it, where does anyone learn about American culture <u>per</u> <u>se?</u> The children of your Asian clients and customers will probably convey the language and oddities of American cultural practices home to their family members, young and old alike. More likely than not, there will be clashes between cultures as well as generations.

How else will our new Asian Americans learn about the Easter bunny, kissing under the Christmas mistletoe, slumber parties, bar and bat mitzvahs, homecoming, and pinching someone for not wearing green on St. Patrick's Day? Who will tell them that they really don't need to call the law enforcement authorities when they wake up one morning and discover that the trees in their front yard have been tee-p'd. Or that when hordes of people come dressed in bizarre attire, knocking on doors, calling "Trick or treat!", they are not begging, but celebrating Halloween.

And who will diplomatically point out to them that it's acceptable to blow one's nose, but never to burp? What is a "burp" anyway?

All those who come to the United States will learn about us from us. We are the ambassadors in today's global community for they will see us as America. By visiting, living, and working here, they will share our joys and sorrows, see our strengths and weaknesses. Our personal and national souls will be laid bare.

When it comes down to basics, it matters not one bit whether you can remember which hand is considered unclean or whether you are going out to have *kim chee*, *sake*, or *sushi*. Asian cultures emphasize human relations. If you stop and think about it, when doing business with peoples of diverse cultures in today's society, we share infinitely more commonalties than have differences. Every human being, whichever country or ethnicity he or she comes from, recognizes and responds to kindness and sincerity, and wants to be treated with dignity.

A savvy businessperson trying to understand and reach today's or the next century's U.S. Asian, or any market, knows that these qualities transcend all cultures.

###

APPENDIX

ASIAN AMERICAN ADVERTISING AND PUBLIC RELATIONS ALLIANCE
1871 Cloverdale Avenue
Los Angeles, CA 90019
Telephone: (213) 39-9088

ASIAN AMERICAN JOURNALISTS ASSOCIATIONS
3921 Wilshire Blvd.
Suite 315
Los Angeles, CA 90010
Telephone: (213) 389-8383

ASIAN AMERICAN MARKET REPORT
8455 Fountain Avenue
Ste. 315
Los Angeles, California 90069
P.O. Box 691889
Los Angeles, 90069-1889, California
Telephone: (213) 650-0102

ASIAN AMERICAN MONITOR
Wesport, Connecticut
Telephone: (714) 756-8880

ASIAN YELLOW PAGES
346 9TH Street
San Francisco, CA 94104
Telephone:)415) 626-4111

ASSOCIATION OF ASIAN PACIFIC AMERICAN ARTISTS
1010 South Flower Street
Room 302
Los Angeles, CA 90015
Telephone: (213) 874-0786

CHINESE CONSUMER YELLOW PAGES AND BUSINESS GUIDE
Asian Media System, Inc.
606 Monterey Pass Road.
#202, Monterey Park, CA 91754

CHINESE YELLOW PAGES AND BUSINESS GUIDE
Davis Media Group
1660 South Amphlett
Suite 122
San Mateo, CA 94402
Telephone: (415) 573-7480   FAX (415) 573-9275

ETHNIC NEWSWATCH
Softline Information
Stamford, Connecticut
Telephone: (203) 968-8878

FILIPINAS
5222 Diamond Heights Blvd.
San Francisco, CA 94131
Telephone: (415) 824-0735

JAPANESE TELEPHONE DIRECTORY AND GUIDE (SO. CALIF.)
Published by Japan Publicity
120 South San Pedro Street
Suite 415
Los Angeles, CA 90012
Telephone: (213)617-1837 FAX (213) 617-7857

KAZN 1300 AM RADIO
800 Sierra MAdre Villa Road
Pasadena, CA
Telephone:

KOREAN BUSINESS DIRECTORY
The Korean Central Daily
690 Wilshire Place
Los Angeles, CA 90005
Telephone: (213) 389-2500 FAX (213) 389-6196

KOREAN BUSINESS DIRECTORY
Published by Korea News
42-22 27th Street
Long Island City, New York 11101
Telephone: (718) 803-0909

KSCI CHANNEL 18
12401 West Olympic Blvd.
Los Angeles, CA 90064

LIFESTYLE USA
Meadow Publications
New York
Telephone: 800-257-5017

MEDIA ACTION NETWORK FOR ASIANS (MANA)
P.O. Box 1881
Santa Monica, CA 90406-1881
Hotline: (213) 486-4433

NCCJ
Southern California Region
635 South Harvard Blvd.
Los Angeles, CA 90005-2596
Telephone: (213) 385-0491

PUBLICITY CLUB OF SOUTHERN CALIFORNIA
5000 Van Nuys Blvd. Suite 300
Sherman Oaks, CA 91403
(213) 872-0525

RAFU SHIMPO
259 South Los Angeles Street
Los Angeles, CA 90012
Telephone (213) 629-2231)

SOUTH BAY (SO. CALIF.) KOREAN BUSINESS DIRECTORY
17813 South Main Street
#112
Gardena, CA 90248
Telephone: (310) 769-5722 FAX (310) 769-4903

UNION OF PAN ASIAN COMMUNITIES
1031 25th Street
San Diego, CA 92102

VERUS GROUP (health care)
613 Taper Drive
Seal Beach, CA 90740
Telephone: (310) 493-9383

YELLOW PAGES JAPAN IN U.S.A.
Yellow Pages Japan Inc. 420 Boyd Street
#502
Los Angeles, CA 90013
Telephone: (213) 680-9101

BIBLIOGRAPHY

Amsden, Alice H. *Asia's Next Giant*. New York: Oxford University Press, 1989.

Archer, Dane. *How to Expand Your S.I.Q. (Social Intelligence Quotient)*. New York: M.Evans and Company, 1980.

Asian Week. *Asians in America: 1990 Census.* San Francisco: Grant Printing House, 1991.

Asian American Studeies Center. *Asian Pacific Directory of Organizations in Greater Los Angeles*. Los Angeles: Asian American Studies Center, UCLA, 1991.

Axtell, Roger. *Do's and Taboos Around the World.* New Yourk: John Wiley and Sons, Inc. --*Do's and Taboos of Hosting International Visitors*. New York: John Wiley and Sons,

Ashcraft, Norman and Scheflen, Albert E. *People Space*. New York: Anchor Books, 1976.

Baldridge, Leticia. *Complete Guide to Executive Manners*. New York: Rawson Assoicates, 1985.

Bartlett, Christopher. *Managing Across Borders: The Transnational Solution*. Sumantra Ghoshal.

Bauer, Helen and Carlquist, Sherwin. *Japanese Festivals*. Garden City, New York:Doubleday, 1965.

Besher, Alexander. *The Pacific Rim Almanac*. New York: Harper Perennial, 1991.

Beuler, William. *Chinese Sayings*. Tokyo, Japan: Charles Tuttle, 1972.

Brannen, Christalyn. *Going to Japan on Business: A Quick Guide to Protocol*, Travel, and Language. Berkeley, CA: Stone Bridge Press, 1991.

Burstein, Daniel. *Yen! Japan's New Financial Empire and Its Threat to America*. New York: Fawcett Columbine, 1990.

Chai, Ch'u and Chai, Winberg. *Confucianism*. Woodbury, New York: Barron's Educational Series, Inc., 1973.

Chambers, Kevin. *A Traveler's Guide to Asian Culture*. Santa Fe: John Muir Publications, 1989.
--*Korean Phrasebook*. Australia: Lonely Planet, 1988.

Chen, A and C. *The Art of War*. Singapore: Graham Brash Ltd.

Chesanow, Neil. *The World-Class Executive*. New York: Rawson Associates, 1985.

Christopher, Robert C. *The Japanese Mind: The Goliath Explained*. New York: Fawcett Columbine, 1983.

Chu, Chin-Ning. *The Asian Mind Game*. New York: Prentice Hall, 1991.
--*The Chinese Mind Game: The Best-Kept Trade Secret of the East*. Beaverton, Oregon: AMC Publishing, 1988.
--*Thick Skin, Black Heart*. 1992.

Cleary, Thomas. *The Japanese Art of War: Understanding the Culture of Strategy*. Boston: Shambala, 1992.
--*The Art of War*. Boston, 1992.

Copeland, Lennie and Griggs, Lewis. *Going International*. New York: Random House. 1985.

Condon, John C. *With Respect to the Japanese: A Guide for Americans*. Yarmouth, Maine: Intercultural Press, 1984.

Cooper, Robert and Nanthapa. *Culture Shock! Thailand*. Singapore: Times Books International, 1990.

Cummings, Jim. *Thai Phrasebook*. Australia: Lonely Planet, 1984.

de Keijzer, Arne J. *China Business Strategies for the 90's*. Berkeley: Pacific View Press, 1992.

De Mente, Boye. *Business Guide to Japan*. Tokyo: Charles Tuttle Yen Books, 1990.
--*Etiquette Guide to Japan*. Tokyo: Charles Tuttle, 1990.
--*Japanese Etiquette and Ethics in Business*. Lincolnwood: NTC, 1991.
--*Korean Etiquette and Ethics in Business*. Lincolnwood: NTC, 1991.

Deutsch, Mitchell F. *Doing Business with the Japanese*. New York: Penguin, 1985.

Draine, Cathie and Barbara Hall. *Culture Shock! Indonesia*. Singapore: Times Books International, 1986.

Eberhard, Wolfram. *A Dictionary of Chinese Symbols: The Hidden Symbols in Chinese Life and Thought*. New York: Routlege, 1986.

Ebrey, Patricia Buckley. *Chinese Civilization and Society: A Sourcebook*. New York: The Free Press, 1981.

Eitel, Ernest. *Feng Shui*. Singapore: Graham Brash, 1984.

Fields, George. *From Bonsai to Levi's*. New York: Mentor Books, 1983.
--*Gucci on the Ginza: Japan's New Consumer Generation*. Tokyo: Kodonsha International, 1989.

Foster, Dean Allen. *Bargaining Across Borders*. New York: McGraw-Hill, 1992.

Gibney, Frank. *Japan: The Fragile Superpower*. Tokyo: Charles E. Tuttle.

Graham, John L. and Sanno, Yoshi. *Smart Bargaining: Doing Business with the Japanese*. New York: Harper Business, 1989.

Griffin, Trenholme and Daggatt, W. Russell. *The Global Negotiator*. New York: Harper Business, 1990.

Hall, Edward T. and Mildred Reed. *Hidden Differences: Doing Business with the Japanese*. New York: Anchor Press/Doubleday, 1987.

Hardwoord, Alan. *Ethnicity and Medical Care*. Cambridge, Massachusetts: Harvard University Press, 1981.

Hendon, Donald and Angeles, Rebecca. *World Class Negotiating*. New York: John Wiley, 1991.

Hsu, Francis L.K. *Americans and Chinese*. Garden City, New York: Doubleday Natural History Press.

Ichheiser, Gustav. *Appearances and Realities*. San Francisco: Josey-Bass, Inc. 1970.

Imai, Masaaki. *Kaizen:Key to Japan's Competitive Success*. New York Random House, 1986.

Ishihara, Shintaro. *The Japan That Can Say No: Why Japan Will Be First Among Equals*. New York: Simon and Schuster, 1991.

Japan Travel Bureau(JTB). *Japan in Your Pocket* (13 volumes)

Kaplan, Frederic M. *The Four Dragons Guidebook*. New York: Eurasia Press (Houghton Mifflin Company), 1991.

Kang, T.W. *Gaishi: The Foreign Company in Japan*. New York: Basic Books, 1990.

Karp, Y.B. *Personal Power*. New York: American Management Association, 1985.

Kester, Carl V. *Japanese Takeovers: The Global Contest for Corporate Control*. Harvard Business School, 1991.

Kleinke, Chris L. *Meeting and Understanding People*. New York: W.H. Freeman and Company, 1986.

Kleinman, Arthur. *Culture and Healing in Asian Societies*. Cambridge, Massachusetts: Schenkman Publishing Company,   1978.

Knoll, Patricia. *Becoming Americans*. Portland, Oregon: Coast to Coast Books, 1982.

Lau, Theodora. *The Handbook of Chinese Horoscopes*. New York: Harper and Row, 1979.

Laurie, Dennis. *Yankee Samurai*. New York: Harper Business, 1992.

Lee, Young O. and Kim, Seong-Kon. *Simple Etiquette in Korea*. England: Paul Norbury Publications, 1988.

Leppert, Paul. *How to Do Business with Chinese*. San Diego: Patton Pacific Press, 1984.

--*Doing Business with the Koreans: A Handbook for Executives*. Sebastopol: Patton Pacific Press Inc.
--*Doing Business in Singapore: A Handbook for Executives*. Sebastopol: Patton Pacific Press Inc.

Lester, Meera. *Writing for the Ethnic Market*. Coopertino, California: Writers Connection, 1991.

Lewis, Michael. *Pacific Rift*. New York: W.W. Norton and Co., 1991.

Li Shijun, Yan Xianju, and Qin Jiarui. *Sun Wu's Art of War and the Art of Business Management*. Hong Kong: Hai Feng, 1990.

Lip, Evelyn. *Feng Shui for Business*. Union City, California: Heian International, Inc., 1990.
   --*Feng Shui: A Layman's Guide to Chinese Geomancy*. Union City, California: Heian, Inc. 1987.
   --*Feng Shui for the Home*. Union City, California: Heian, Inc., 1990.

Los Angeles County Commission on Human Relations. *How to Communicate Better with Clients, Customers, and Workers Whose English is LImited*. 320 West Temple Street, Suite 1184,   Los Angeles, CA 90012.

Lu, David. *Inside Corporate Japan: The Art of Fumble-Free Management*. Tokyo: Charles E. Tuttle, 1987.

Lu, Henry C. *Chinese Sytem of Food Cures: Prevention and Remedies*. New York: Sterling Press, 1986.

Machovec, Frank. *I Ching: The Book of Changes*. Mt. Vernon: Peter Pauper Press, 1971.

MacLeod, Roderick. *China Inc. How to Do Business with the Chinese*. New York: Bantam Books, 1988.

Makkai, Adam. *A Dictionary of American Idioms*. Hauppauge, New York: Barron's, 1987.

March, Robert. *The Japanese Negotiator: Subtlety and Strategy Beyond Western Logic*. New York: Kodansha International, 1988.
   --*Honoring the Customer:Marketing and Selling to the Japanese*. New York: John Wiley, 1991.

Matsumoto, Michihiro. *The Unspoken Way: Haragei: Silence in Japanese Business and Society*. New York: Kodansha International, 1989.

Mizutani, Osamu and Nobuko. *How to Be Polite in Japanese*. Tokyo: Japan Times.

Molloy, John T. *The New Dress for Success*. New York: Warner Books, 1988.

Montgomery, Stephen L. *Profitable Pricing Strategies*. New York: McGraw-Hill, 1988.

Moran, Robert. *Getting Your Yen's Work: How to Negotiate with Japan, Inc*. Houston: Gulf Publishing Company, 1985.
   --*Managing Cultural Differences*. Houston: Gulf Publishing, 1991.

Morgan, James C. and Jeffrey. *Cracking the Japanese Market*. New York: the Free Press.

Morsbach, Helmet. *The Japanese Travelmate: An A to Z Phrase Book of Useful Words and Important Phrases.* San Francisco: Chronicle Books, 1989.

Musashi, Miyamoto. *A Book of Five Rings: The Classic Guide to Strategy.* New York: The Overlook Press, Bantam, 1982.

Munan, Heidei. *Culture Shock! Malaysia.* Singapore: Times Books International, 1991.

Naisbitt, John and Aburdene, Patricia. *Megatrends.* New York: Avon, 1990.

National Conference of Christians and Jews. *Asian Pacific Americans.* 635 South Harvard Street, Los Angeles, CA 90005: NCCJ, 1989.

Nevins, Thomas J. *Labor Pains and the Gaijin Boss: Hiring, Managing, and Firing the Japanese.* Tokyo: Japan Times, 1985.

Ni, Maoshing. *The Tao of Nutrition.* Malibu, California: The Shrine of the Eternal Breath of Tao, 1989.

Omae, Kenichi. *Beyond International Borders.* New York: Kodansha International.

--*The Mind of the Strategist: The Art of Japanese Business.* New York: McGraw-Hill, 1982.

Ouchi, William. *Theory 2: How American Business Can Meet the Japanese Challenge.* New York: Avon Books, 1981.

Palmer, Martin. *T'ung Shu: The Ancient Chinese Almanac.* Boston: Shambala, 1986.

Pierre, Do-Dinh. *Confucius and Chinese Humanism.* New York: Funk and Wagnalls, 1969.

Press, Peter Pauper. *The Wisdom of Confucius.* Mount Vernon: Peter Pauper, 1963.

Roces, Alfredo and Grace. *Culture Shock! A Guide to Customs and Etiquette: Philippines.* Portland: Graphic Arts Publishing Center, 1985.

Rossbach, Sarah. *Interior Design with Feng Shui.* New York: E.P. Dutton, 1987.

--*Feng Shui: The Chinese Art of Placement.* New York: E.P. Dutton, 1987.

Rowland, Diana. *Japanese Business Etiquette: A Practical Guide to Success with the Japanese.* New York: Warner Books, 1985.

Sinclair, Kevin and Po Yee, Iris Wong. *Culture Shock! China*. Singapore: Times Books International, 1990.

Skinner, Stephen. *The Living Earth Manual of Feng Shui: Chinese Geomancy*. Singapore: Graham Brash, 1982.

Snowden, Sondra. *The Global Edge: How Your Company Can Win in the International Marketplace*. New York: Simon and Schuster,   1986.

Stanley, Thomas J. *Seliing to the Affluent*. Homewood, Illinois: Business One Irwin. 1991.

Stewart, Edward C. *American Cultural Patterns*. Yarmouth, Maine: Intercultural Press, 1972.

Stewart, Majabelle and Faux, Marian. *Executive Etiquette*. New York: St. Martin's Press, 1979.

Stonebridge Press. *Going to Japan on Business*.

Takaki, Ron. *Strangers from a Different Shore*. New York: Penguin, 1989.

Tonkin, Derek. *Simple Etiquette in Thailand*. England: Paul Norbury Publications, 1990.

Union of Pan Asian Communities. *Understanding the Pan Asian Client*. Book II. 1031 25th Street, San Diego, CA 92102. San Diego, 1980.

Van Wolferen, Karen. *The Enigma of Japanese Power*. Vintage Books.

United States Commission on Civil Rights. *Civil Rights Issues Facing Asian Americans in the 1990s*. Washington, D.C.: 1992.

Wall Street Journal *Guides to Business Travel: Pacific Rim*. New York: Fodor's Travel Publication, 1991.

Walters, Derek. *Feng Shui Handbook*. Hammersmith, London: Aquarian Press, 1991.

    --*Feng Shui: Perfect Placing for Your Happiness and Prosperity.* Singapore: AsiaPac, 1988.

Waters, Dan. *21st. Century Management: Keeping Ahead of the Japanese and Chinese*. New York: Simon and Schuster, 1991.

Williams, C.A.S. *Outlines of Chinese Symbolism and Art Motives*. Tokyo: Charles Tuttle, 1974.

Winchester, Simon. *Pacific Rising; The Emergence of a New World Culture*, 1991.

Wirkland, Erik. *International Marketing*. New York: McGraw-Hill, 1986.

Yuan, Goa. *Lure the Tiger Out of the Mountains: The 36 Strategems of Ancient China*. New York: Simon and Schuster, 1991.

Zimmerman, Mark. *How to Do Business with the Japanese: A Strategy for Success*. New York: Random House, 1985.

INDEX

C

D

P

Papua New Guinea 32
Patience 90, 101, 102, 169, 170
Pennsylvania 40, 56, 61
Pepsi Cola 2, 113, 118
Personal space 147
Philippines 32, 36, 49, 83, 145, 206
Photographs 55, 91, 110, 111, 151, 155, 191, 193
Pilipino 36
Post-Intelligence, Seattle 54
Proverbs 41, 46, 190

R

Rafu Shimpo 55, 199
Refugees 31, 48, 49, 104
Relationships 39, 69, 100, 140, 156, 157, 161, 167, 170, 171, 173, 176, 177, 178, 179, 187, 193
Rhode Island 61

S

Samoa 36, 27
San Francisco 41, 49, 51, 63, 92
Sansei 46
Scientific American 77
Scott Act 48
Seattle 54
Second wave 49
Selling 21, 44, 96, 114, 122, 183, 186, 205
Sha 129
Shinto 34
Shoes 84, 102, 152, 153
Sikh 34
Singapore 37, 72, 83, 121, 130, 150, 204
Smile 89, 150, 151, 155, 171
South Bay Korean Business Directory 51, 199
South Carolina 61
Southern California 23, 26, 51, 54, 92, 113, 118, 121, 127, 130, 199
SRI Research Center, Inc. 5
Stereotypes 42, 43, 44, 45, 110

Contacts

Notes